Don't Sweat the Details!

Easy Watercolor Techniques for Beginners

by Davida Schulman

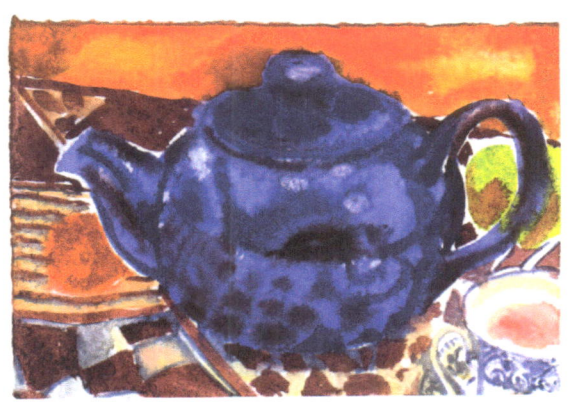

ISBN 10: 09979661-0-6

ISBN 13: 978-0-9979661-0-7

Contents

Introduction

Watercolor is a most popular painting medium. It has many advantages. It's very portable, easily carried outdoors or along on a vacation. Watercolor requires no volatile solvents for cleanup and produces no irritating fumes. One can create watercolors in small spaces. An artist may walk away from a project and return to it easily with a quick rinse of brushes. And if you forget to rinse your brushes, they are not ruined. Dry watercolor paint easily rinses out of brushes with plain soap and water.

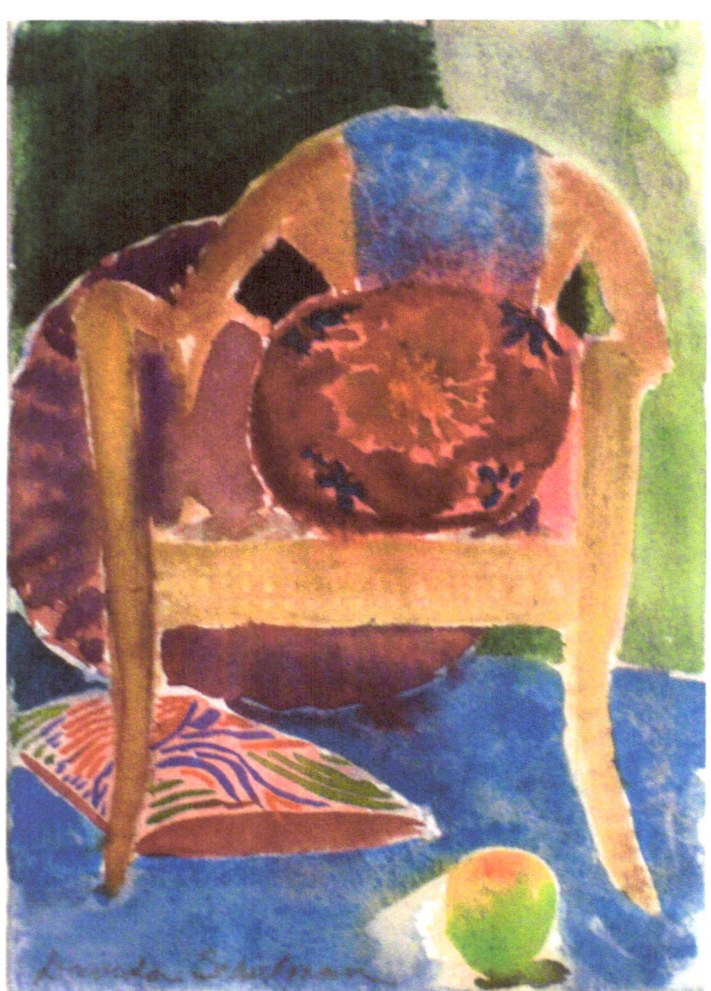

Wicker Chair, Watercolor on Masa Paper, 7.5x3.75"

Aside from these practical advantages, there are a number of aesthetic advantages to watercolor painting. If you appreciate brilliant hues, watercolor is for you! The optical mix of transparent watercolor layers on white paper can be glowingly luminous and the results incredibly fast to execute. Effects that might take hours with oils or acrylics sometimes will take only seconds with watercolor.

So, why would anyone use anything else but watercolor? Perhaps it is because watercolor is often described as a most difficult painting material. It is, however, no more difficult than any other painting material. It's just different than the others in that it is transparent, while gouache and acrylics are more opaque. Opaque materials permit overpainting for correction and changes, while overpainting with watercolor typically ends in an unsatisfactory, overworked result. The issue of fluidity with watercolor often makes it seem uncontrollable—another of the greatest difficulties for a beginner to master.

This book will guide you through a series of easy steps in accumulating the knowledge necessary to overcome all these seemingly overwhelming difficulties. The first step is to provide you with the freedom to play without concern for "wasting" expensive materials. This doesn't mean you should work with poor-quality materials, just less-expensive foundation materials. Even the most expensive watercolor paints remain cost-effective, as they go a long way.

I have been painting with watercolor for nearly thirty years. I also work in acrylics and oils, but watercolor is still my preferred medium. Until about ten years ago, I used 100 percent cotton, rag paper exclusively. Then, on a whim, I bought some masa, an acid-free, Japanese printmaking paper. It was on sale—less than a dollar for a sheet measuring 21" x 31", nearly the same size as my favorite and expensive rag paper (22" x 30") that retails for about $12 per sheet. I thought, "I can play with this paper and experiment without feeling guilty!" The potential for ruining a $12 sheet of paper with wild abandon offended my frugal soul.

Masa paper, at first glance, appears to be thin and flimsy, but it is very tough and hard to tear. The two sides are finished differently with one side smooth and shiny, while the other is soft and slightly fuzzy. I soon found out that I preferred the fuzzy side. That fuzziness seemed to inhibit the spread of paint on the wet surface. As soon as I started playing with it, I was hooked.

I discovered that I liked working with masa while it is wet. I quickly came to love the soft, atmospheric effects that resulted. I could play off different densities of pigment against each other and lift color easily. I could even wash all the color off the paper as long as it was wet, and yet still use many of the watercolor tricks I had learned to use while painting on rag paper.

Masa also put me in exactly the right place for painting. While the paper is wet, I am forced to be a generalist. As the paper dries, I can then refine for more detail. Focusing on detail at the outset is a particularly poor strategy, and quite common among beginners. One cannot see the forest for the leaves. Even as an experienced artist, I still fall back into that trap on occasion. Starting out with wet paper prevents that. If I begin to go for detail, any mark I make just dissipates into the water on the surface.

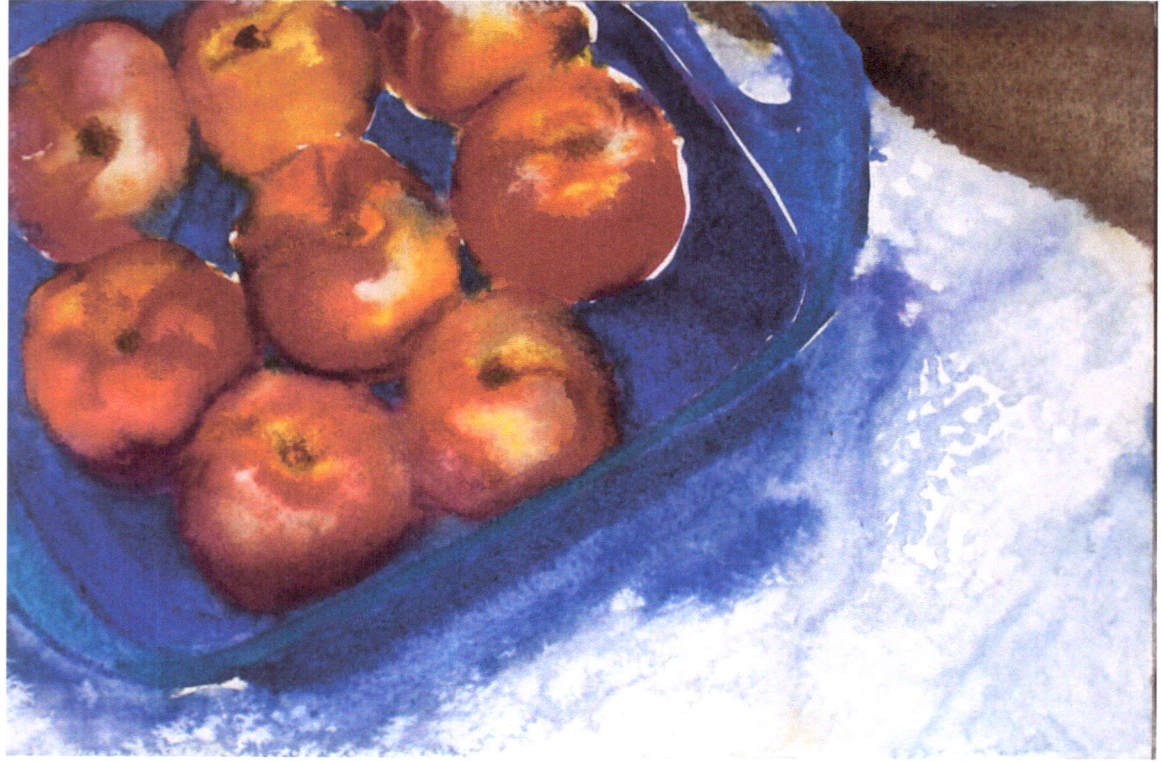

Eight Nectarines, Watercolor on Masa Paper, 10.5x15.5"

Masa also prevents you from becoming obsessed with corrections. The compulsive need to "fix" a stroke leads to overworking the surface, causing the fuzzy texture of masa paper to pill up like c cheap sweater. Masa teaches me to learn from the natural consequences of any bad habits. By enduring the consequences, you, too, will break from bad habits. I never know how a masa watercolor will dry. I am always surprised by the happy accidents and the not-so-happy accidents. They teach me that I can't control everything. The element of surprise makes it much more fun anyway.

If you have never painted with watercolor, the following information will point the way toward gaining painting experience by playing freely and without guilt.

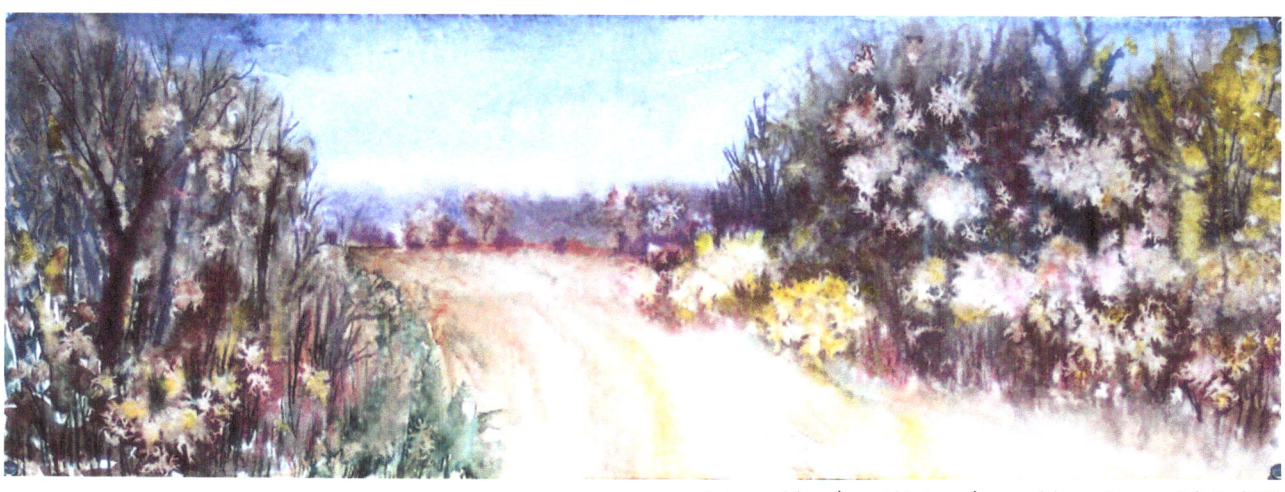

Autumn Meadow, Watercolor on Masa Paper, 10.5x31"

Materials

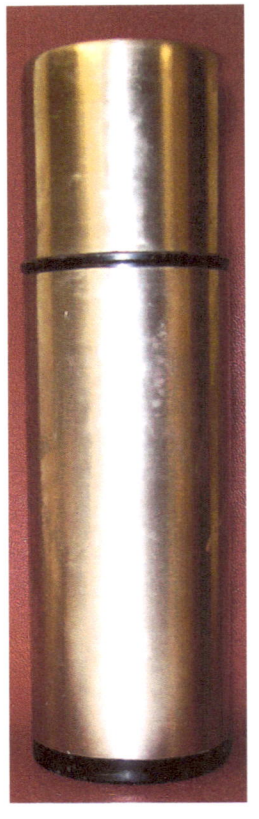

From the top right:
- pressurizing water misting bottle
- collapsing water jug
- salt containers

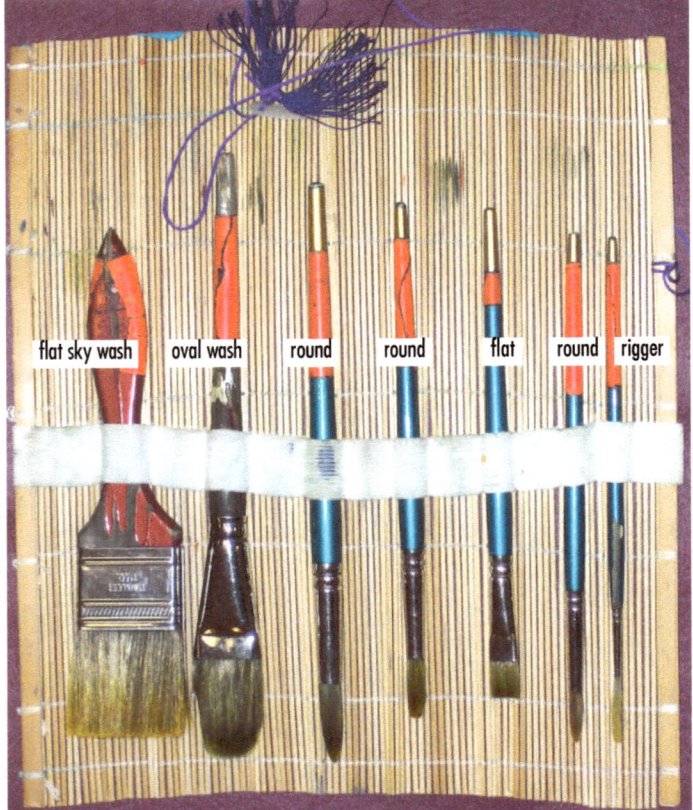

flat sky wash | oval wash | round | round | flat | round | rigger

Brushes from the left: 2 1/2" flat sky wash, 1" oval wash (filbert), 3/8" round, 3/16" round, 1/2" flat, 1/4" round, rigger. Shown in their bamboo carrier. The red tape on the handles are for times when I'm outdoors painting. If I drop a brush in the grass, I'll be able to see it easily. At least that's the theory.

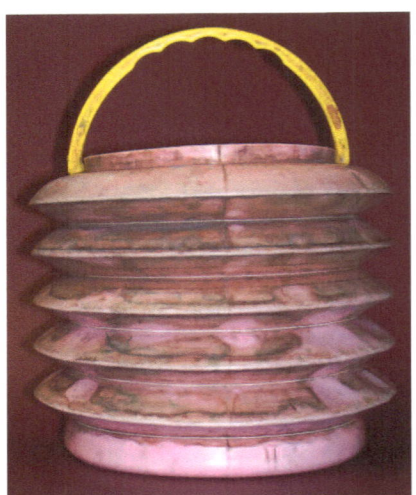

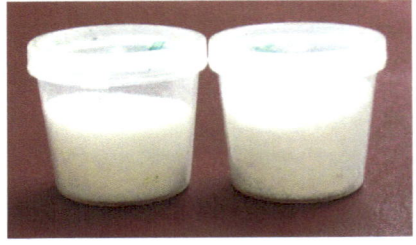

Masa Paper: I order my masa by mail. It comes in ten-sheet packs. I order it 100 sheets at a time because I found the cost of shipping a ten-pack sheet is more than the cost of the paper. Pool your orders with friends and divide the 100-sheet packs. If the order is large enough, the shipping might be free. That's a considerable savings.

Watercolor Brushes: Good-quality synthetic or synthetic blend brushes are my preference. They retain their shapes well. Pictured are my watercolor brushes, shown for size. There is no standard for sizes. The numbers on each manufacturer's brushes are simply the standard sizes for that manufacturer. I have had some of my brushes for over twenty years. If you take care of them, they will provide you with the same level of service. Choose a brush with enough spring that it will return to its shape after each stroke.

Make sure you don't leave your brushes soaking in the water pot. Soaking will cause the wooden handles to swell, which will stretch the metal ferrule so it remains loose after the handle has dried. Once the wooden brush handle is dry and returned to its original size, the ferrule will have stretched so much there is little that can be done to tighten it again. The slight jiggle that results makes it impossible for you to ever again place the bristles of your brush exactly where you want them, and the brush is ruined.

> 1-2½" flat wash
>
> 1-1"oval wash
>
> 1-¾" oval wash (filbert)
>
> 1-⅜" round
>
> 1-½" flat
>
> 1-¼" round
>
> 1-rigger or liner

Bamboo Brush Holder: Transporting your collection of brushes in a bamboo brush holder allows you to place them in your bag with the brush ends facing downward. This allows the water to drain out from the brush and prevents the dreaded loose ferrule effect. Make sure you have a brush holder with an elastic band to hold your brushes in place so they don't end up resting on their bristle tips.

*A list of resources where masa paper can be purchased is on page 42.

Watercolor paints: A good-quality, student grade paint is a perfect choice. The difference between student grade and artist grade watercolor is the pigment load and the fineness of the pigment grind. Pigment load refers to the proportion of pigment to the fluid (carrier) in which the pigment granules are suspended. The greater the pigment load, the better. The two grades are compatible with each other, so once you decide watercolor is for you, you can add artist grade watercolors to your supply without any concern. I use artist grade paint precisely for the pigment load, especially with the cadmium reds. I want a very dense paint, so I get red, not pink, with the first pass of a well-loaded brush.

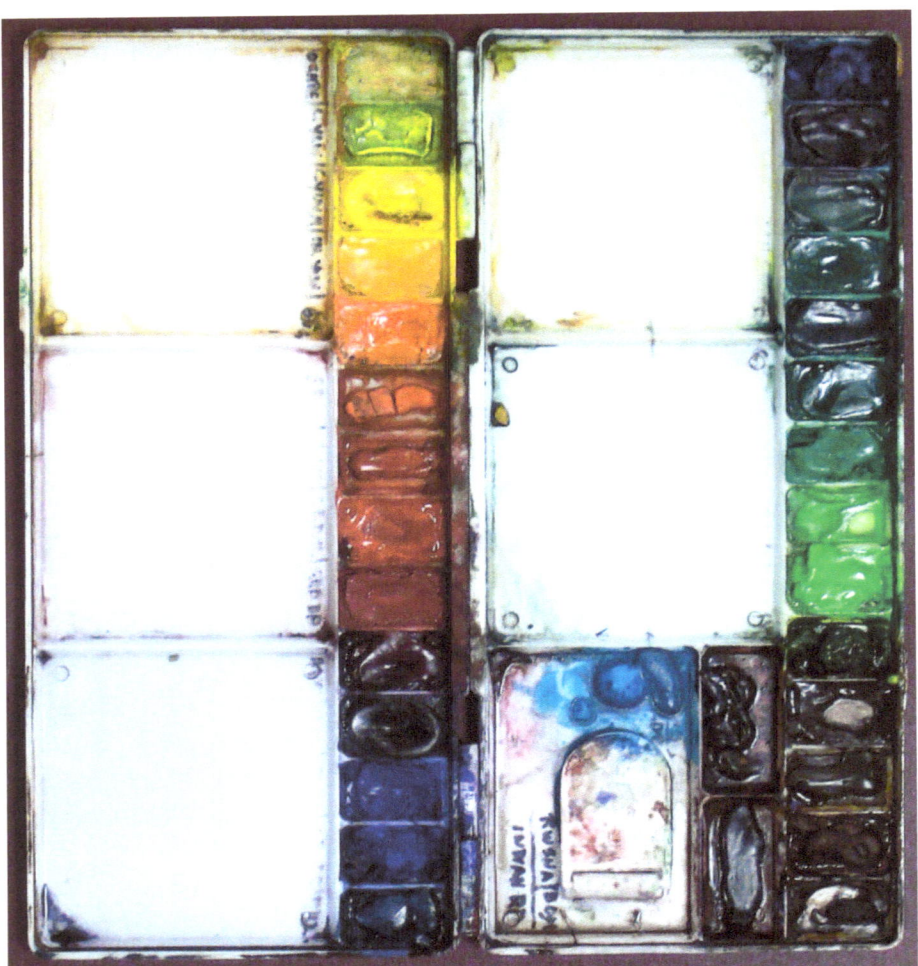

My 12x11" Holbein style folding palette has 30 wells. I have several palettes with different color combinations for different subject matters. My landscape palette has more greens. My figure painting palette has fewer greens. I also set my paints out from cool to warm. Yellows are generally cool on the left to orange to reds to violets to blue, etc. all my colors are arranged that way. I usually have a few wells left over. Those end up being filled with the oddballs; the pigments I might acquire after the palette has been laid out.

English Watercolor Palette:

New Gamboge,   Indian Red (red oxide),   Indigo

An expanded basic palette added to the English Palette:

(C) or (W) indicates a cool or warm version of a hue

Blues\Green:	Ultramarine Blue,(C)	Phthalo Blue,(W)	Pthalo Green(W)
Reds:	Cad. Red Lt.,(W)	Alizarin Crimson,(C)	
Yellows:	Lemon Yellow,(C)	Cad. Yellow Mdm.,(W)	
Earth Tones:	Burnt Umber,(C)	Burnt Sienna,(W)	Yellow Ochre

Grumbacher Academy, Van Gogh, Winsor and Newton Cotman Watercolors, are three brands that are of a good quality for beginners. I like the Cotman colors the least. There is an additive that gives the colors a milky, semi-opaque quality that does not appeal to me. However, you choose what seems right for you. Art suppliers have sales on watercolor paints just when we are all ready to go outside in early spring. That's when I replenish my supplies and place an order with a friend. That order is usually large enough for free, priority shipping.

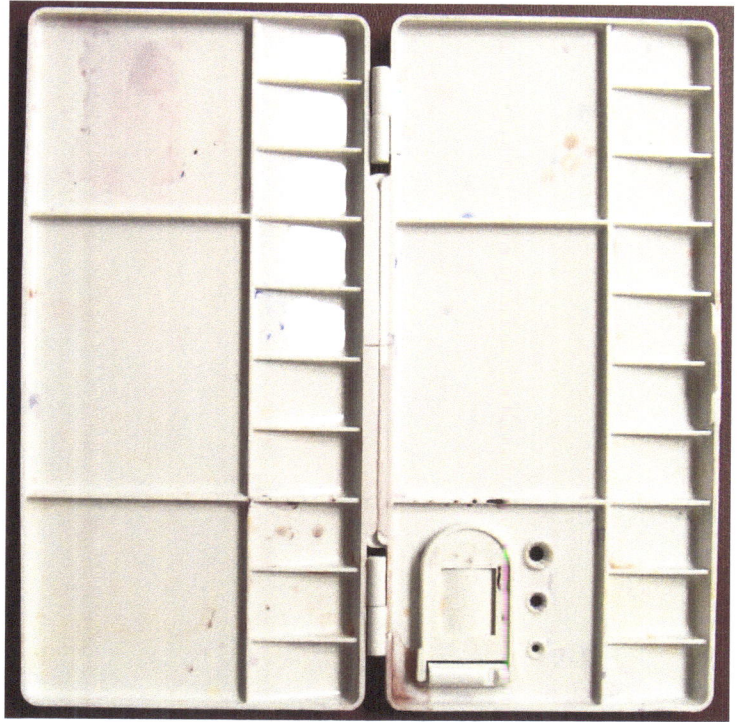

This an 8x8" palette with 20 wells. It is ideal for travel. A palette should never be as clean as this one. Better a creative mess than tidy idleness.

English watercolors: English watercolors: An English palette consists of Indian red, gamboge (yellow) and indigo (blue). Indian red (also known as English red) is a red oxide mined in India. Venetian red is also a red oxide. The character of the red changes with mining location. Venetian red is warmer than Indian red. Indian red has a violet cast that renders it cooler.

English watercolors are named for a group of English watercolorists including John Consatble, John Sell Cotman, Paul Sandby, and J. M. W. Turner. Together, they transformed the status of watercolor from a sketch-and-study medium to that of a medium for finished works of art. These pigments were among the only ones available at the time for field work, making up a primary triad. They can produce a complete color range, though much less brilliant than the one to which we are now accustomed. This is a limited color set, the purpose of which is to keep a beginner from becoming overwhelmed by too many choices. You can always add to it as you feel the need.

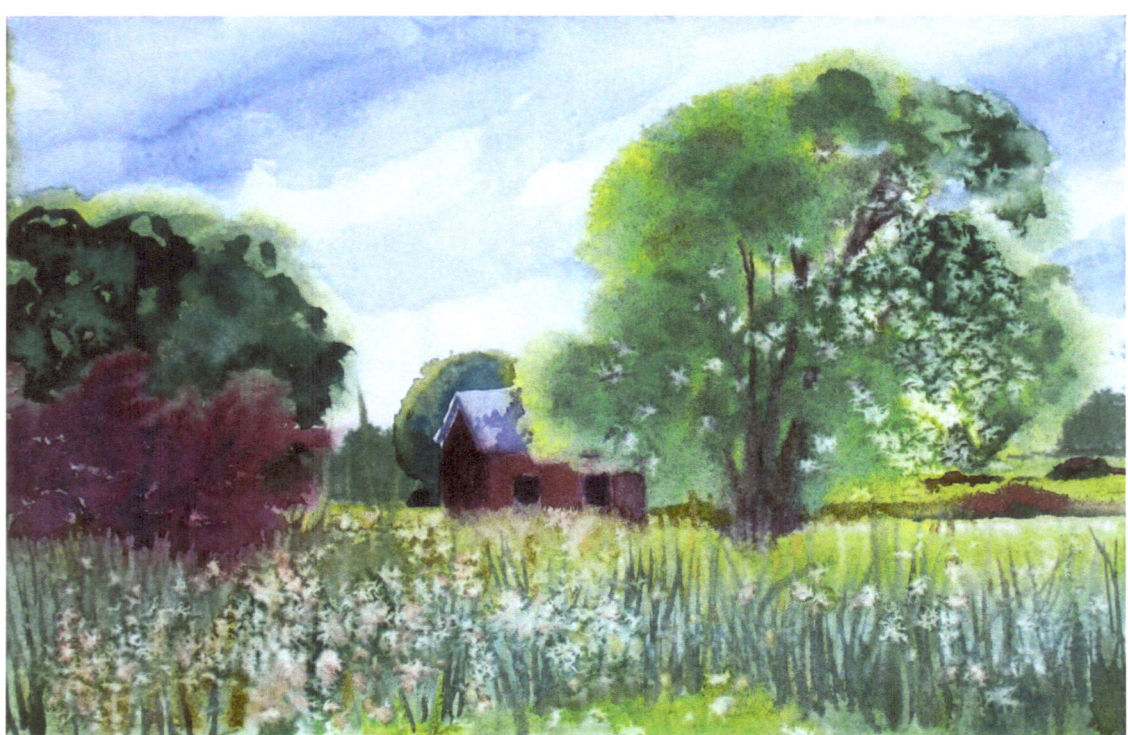

View from Gravel Pit Road, Watercolor on Masa Paper, 10.5x15.5"

Holbein style folding palette: This style of palette enhances the portability of watercolor. It folds compactly and easily fits into a bag or tackle box. Fill the palette and have a full palette ready whenever you need it. Beginners tend to be very stingy with paint. The beauty of watercolor is you can allow the paint to dry and still be able to use it again and again. Just re-wet it.

Spray bottle: I use an aluminum olive oil mister. I can pump the bottle to pressurize it for a continuous spray of water. Make sure the one you select has never been used for olive oil and reserve it for watercolor use only.

Water containers: Large yogurt or cottage cheese containers are ideal.

Paper towels: If possible, select a plain brand with no embossed or printed patterns (Viva).

Salt: Fine table salt and coarse-grained kosher salt in small containers. Salt packets from a fast food restaurant are particularly convenient.

An 18x24" water-impermeable board: Plastic-coated, tempered Masonite is available from your local home project store. It is called tile board. Ask for plain white, smooth tile board. I typically use a piece of old Plexiglas. It's thin and light weight.

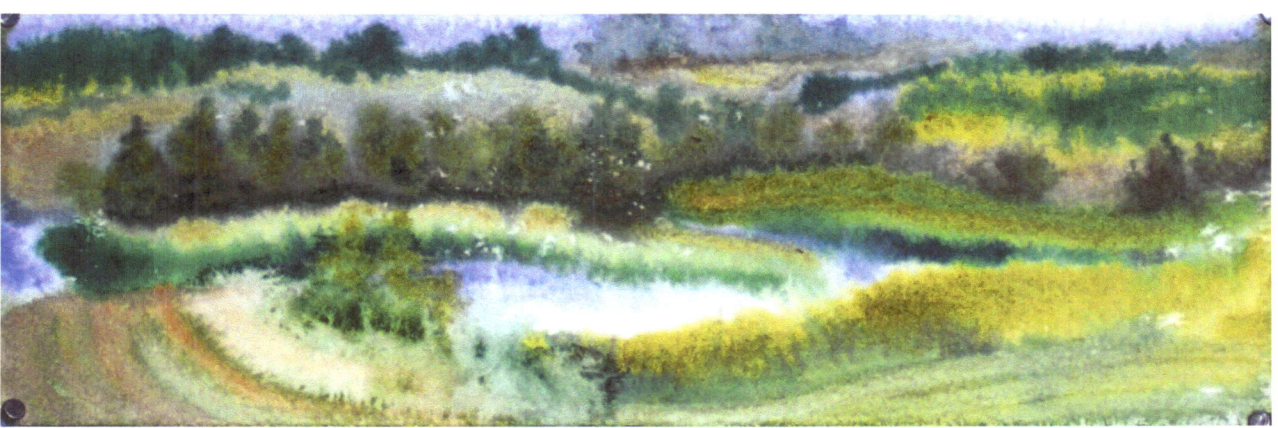

Nebraska Landscape, Watercolor on Masa Paper, 5.5x14"

Paper & Mounting

Masa paper comes in one size, 21" x 31", which is very close to a standard sheet of rag paper (22"x 30"). I find that a full-sized sheet of masa is too daunting for a beginner. It's best to start small and work up to larger sizes when learning to use new materials.

I slice my masa paper into smaller sizes. Remember that masa is much tougher than it appears and difficult to tear. Rather than a scissors or paper cutter, I like to use an old, serrated, bread knife to cut my paper for the effect it has on the edges. I take three or four sheets at a time and carefully fold them in half while stacked together. Using the fold, I slide my knife between the inside layer and cut along the fold. (See image) Then, depending on what sizes I want, I repeat the process with the

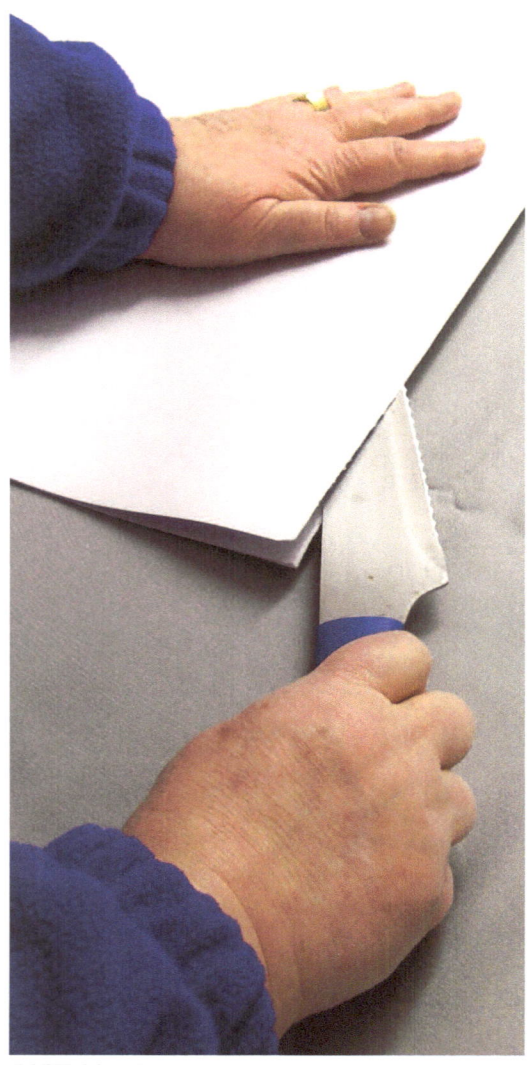

A serrated knife does a great job tearing through very thin, but very tough paper. You can use any serrated knife you have. I like the appearance of the edge left by the knife. It looks deckled.

pieces I have already cut. The effect of using the serrated knife mimics the look of a deckle edge—named after the kind of irregular thin edge made by paper slurry leaking under a deckle frame during the paper-making process. See the image of the teapot on page 20 for the effect of masa cut with a serrated knife.

Below are examples of sizes resulting from this paper-cutting process—five sizes that I can choose from. The numbers correspond with the sizes at right.

1. full sheet : 21 x 31"
2. half sheet: 21 x 15½"
3. quarter sheet: 15½ x 10½"
4. eighth sheet: 10½ x 7¾"
5. sixteenth sheet: 5¼ x 7¾"

The trimmed paper sizes are all very workable and at a cost well under $1.00. Let the unfettered play commence!

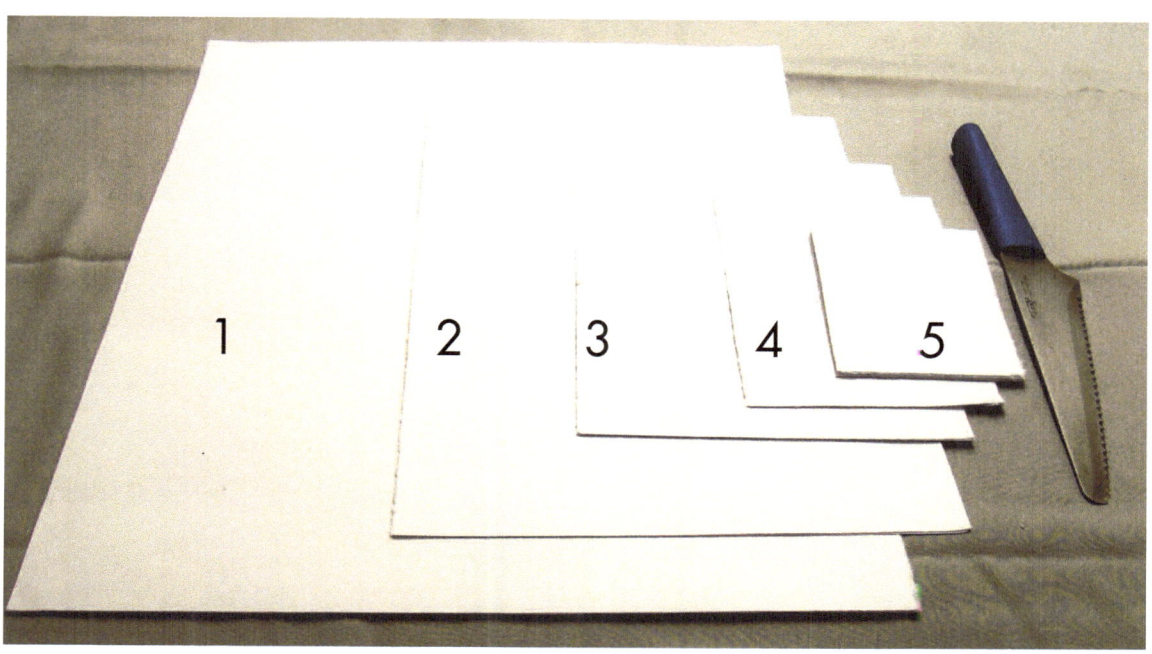

Below are the results of my paper tearing. There are now 5 sizes for painting.
The numbers correspond with the numbered sizes seen above

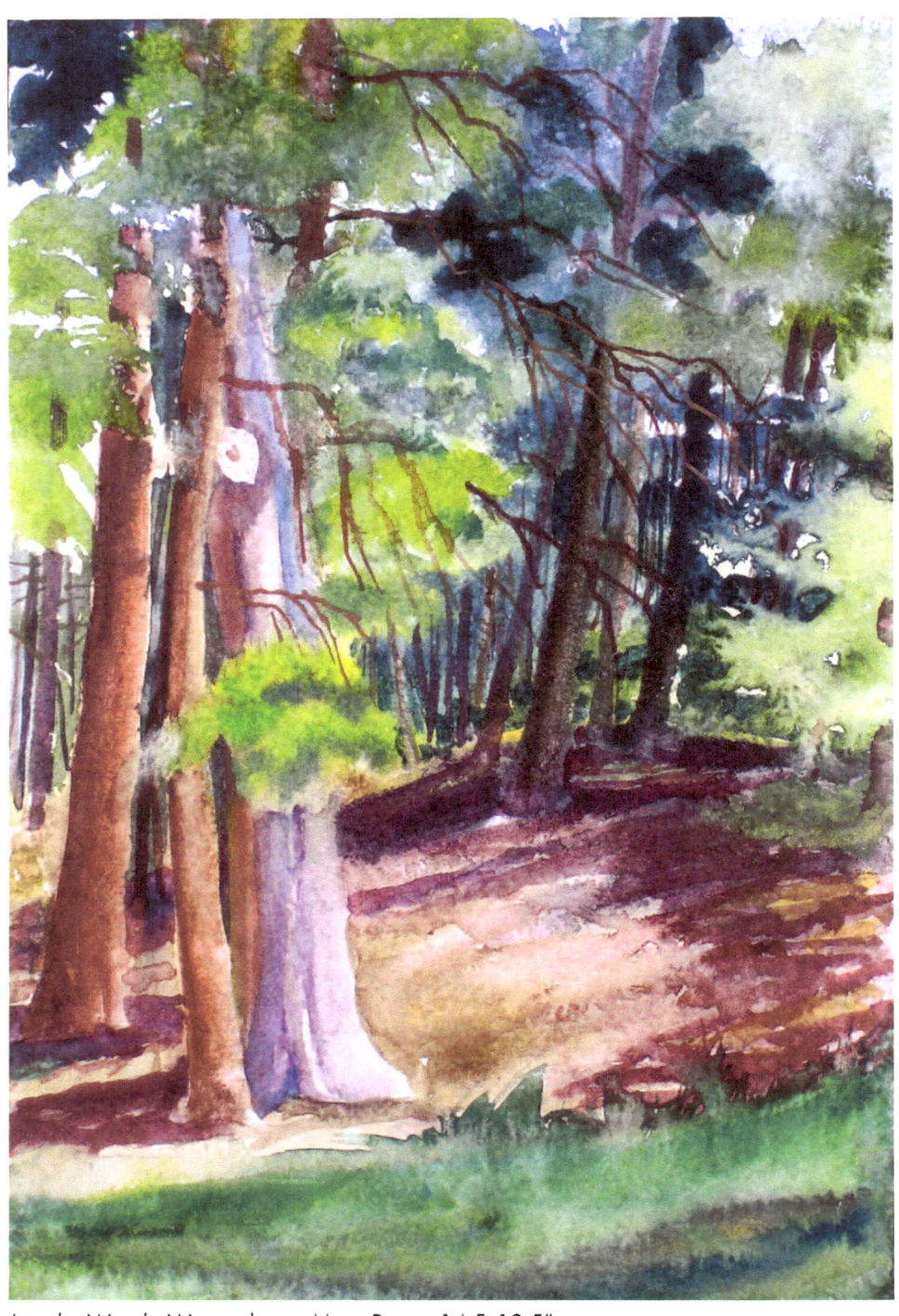

Into the Woods, Watercolor on Masa Paper, 14.5x10.5"

Mounting the paper: You will need a water-impermeable mounting board, a spray-bottle filled with water, and a single sheet of paper in whatever size you have selected.

Step 1: Evenly spray the surface of your mounting board with water from your spray bottle.

Step 2: Evenly spray the back side (the shiny side) of the masa paper.

Step 3: As the masa paper begins to curl towards the toothy front side, place the shiny back side down on the mounting board with the center of the curl in the center of the board. Smooth the paper down and out, working from the center to the edges. You must proceed rather quickly to prevent the paper from buckling.

Step 4: After you have flattened out the masa paper, evenly spray the remaining front side with water. This will make both sides of the paper evenly damp to further prevent buckling.

If you can submerge the paper in water completely, that's even better. It allows the water to evenly wet the paper and makes it readily lay flat on your mounting board. Outdoors it's not possible, so you will need to master both mounting methods. The mounting process will require a little bit of practice to perfect, but it becomes easy once you develop a sense of how much water is needed. Try not to make the front side too wet. It should be slightly wetter than just damp. If it gets puddy, use paper toweling to blot the surface. Lay out a flat sheet of paper towel and blot the surface to lift off the excess water. Don't rub the wet paper! That will damage the surface of the masa and cause it to pill.

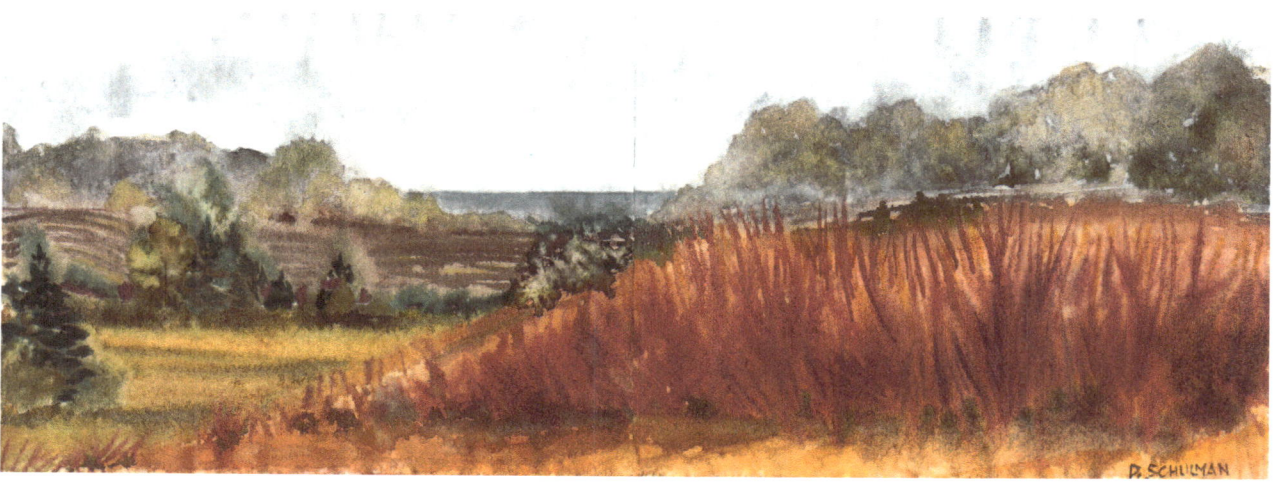

Early Spring, Watercolor on Masa Paper, 7.5x21"

Color Theory & Pigments

Color Chart

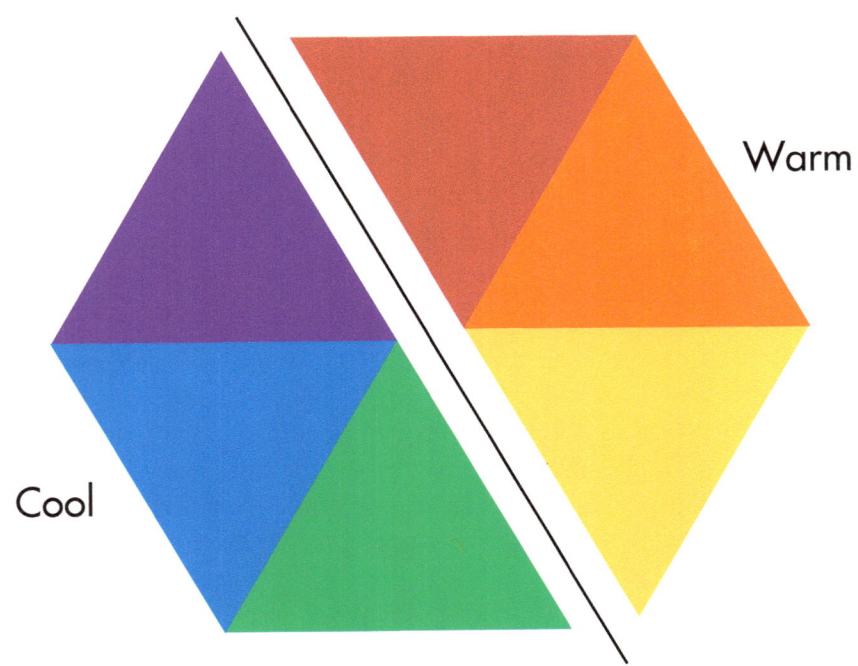

For the sake of beginners, let's assume you don't know much about color theory. Despite my efforts, any written explanation, no matter how expansive, must remain cursory since color is a perceptual sensation. The sensation must be interpreted through the eyes and brain, and then to the hands of the artist. That prompts sensory experience creates the conditions for learning to think visually.

Below is a basic explanation of secondary and complementary colors. Technically, the term "color" is an overarching category for all color. "Hue" is the correct term for a singular instance of any color. We say red is a color and green is a color when they are, in fact, each an individual hue. However, we typically use the term "color" instead of "hue" most of the time. Since that's the way most of us have come to understand it, that's how I will refer to them—as colors.

The primary color triad consists of red, yellow and blue. These colors cannot be created on your palette through mixing. Before the nineteenth century, primary colors had to be found in nature. Brilliant blue was once only obtained, very expensively, by grinding lapis lazuli. Indigo was less expensive, but much less brilliant. Red was mined as carnelian, red oxides, red lead or vermillion, or it was derived from the madder plant or crushed cochineal insects. Yellow was obtained from mineral deposits of yellow ochre.

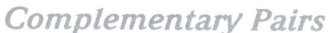

Complementary Pairs

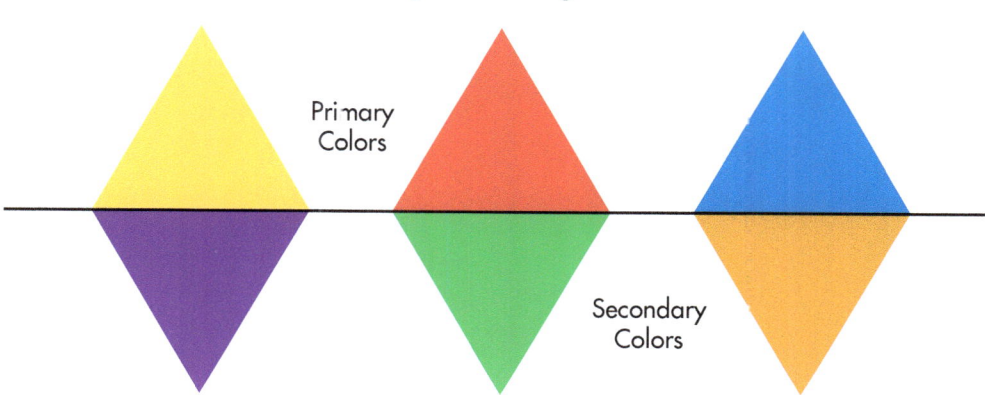

Primary
Colors

Secondary
Colors

During the nineteenth century, chemists discovered how to synthesize some of these brilliant hues. Ultramarine blue was once only obtained by grinding lapis lazuli. The French government offered a prize in 1824 for a less-costly blue pigment. A by product of glassmaking was found to be similar in composition to lapis. This became French ultramarine blue. The cadmium red, yellow, and chromes yellow cobalt blues and greens came afterward. It was the beginning of the modern availability of the intense, pure colors we now experience and take for granted. Complementary colors are colors that have the most extreme contrast in temperature (cool/warm) and value (light/dark). Each color in the complementary pair makes its mate appear to be more intense. The word "complementary" indicates a completion. To have a complementary color pairing, one must have all three primary colors present simultaneously in the form of one secondary color (i.e. green, orange, or violet) and one primary color (red, blue, or yellow). The two primary colors that are combined in the makeup of a secondary color are complemented, or completed, by the remaining primary color in the triad.

Complementary pairs are as follows (See chart above):

Green (yellow and blue) + Red

Orange (yellow and red) + Blue

Violet (red and blue) + Yellow

On a color wheel, the complementary pairs are directly opposite each other. It's much easier to figure out what combinations are complements by noting the two primary colors that comprise a secondary color, then simply complete the triad with the remaining primary color. Trying to visualize a color wheel in your mind's eye is much more difficult. You might also have a split complementary color scheme, which is comprised of colors that are close to, but on either side of the colors directly opposite a singular color on the color wheel.

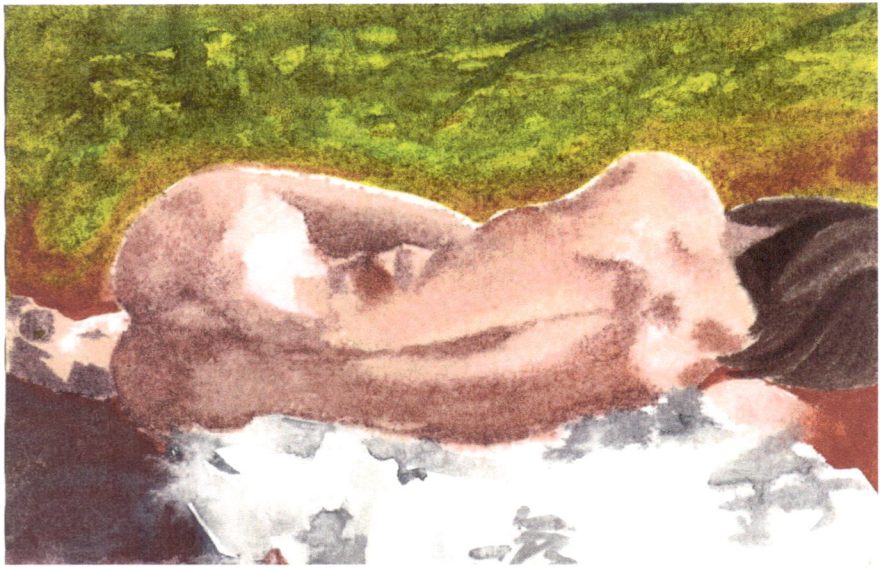

On Her Side, Watercolor on Masa Paper, 5.25x5.75".

Complementary Color Schemes:

Each of these paintings has a complementary color scheme. The upper painting has a green/red relationship. The lower painting has an orange/blue relationship.

Neither painting is totally done with two complementary colors but, the complements noted are dominant in each piece.

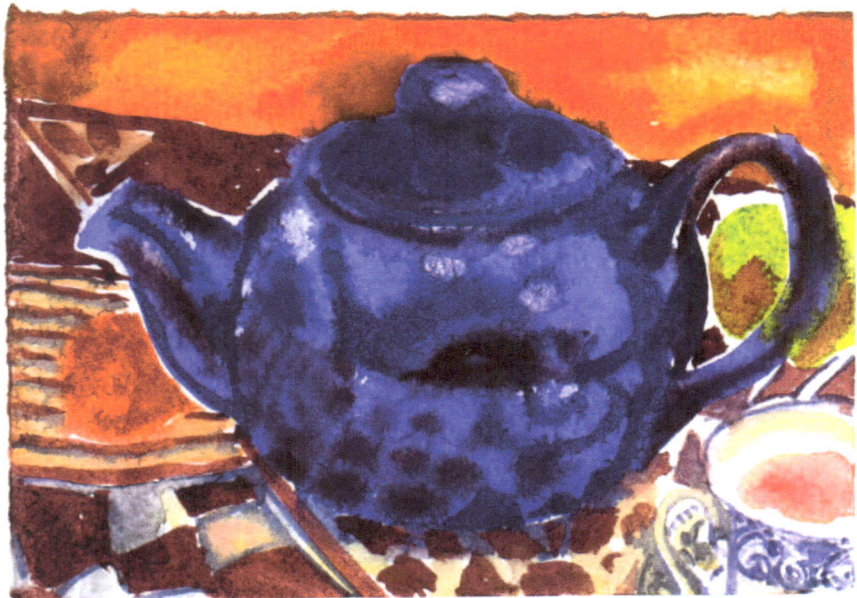

Blue Teapot, Watercolor on Masa Paper, 3.875x5.25"

The English watercolor palette that I have listed under the materials category is an "old fashioned" primary triad. The secondary colors green, orange, and violet (purple) can be mixed with these three primary pigments. Complementary colors can then be used to make each color seem more or less intense. The proximity of the complements make for the effect. For instance, look at the cool side of the color chart and the adjacent blue and violet triangles. Then, look at the violet/yellow complementary pair and see how the contrast between the two is enhanced by their being next to each other. English Red or Indian Red is an iron oxide (rust). Gamboge was once the product of cows fed yellow mango leaves, then harvesting the yellow pigment from the cow urine. New gamboge reproduces that hue, so thankfully we no longer need to paint with cow's urine. Indigo is an ancient, blue vegetable dye. It's the same color as our blue jeans.

Each of these pigments has a different density, with iron oxide having the greatest density and weight, and indigo having the least density and weight. The differences in the density of pigments can be worked against each other to greater effect. For instance, red oxide is so heavy that it will literally push a wet indigo wash aside and replace it on the paper! If the indigo is dry, red oxide is so opaque that it will cover the indigo blue. The cadmiums, cobalts and earth tones also share this same kind of density. Dye colors such as phthaloes, quinacridones, and alizarins are dyes which are transparent like indigo.

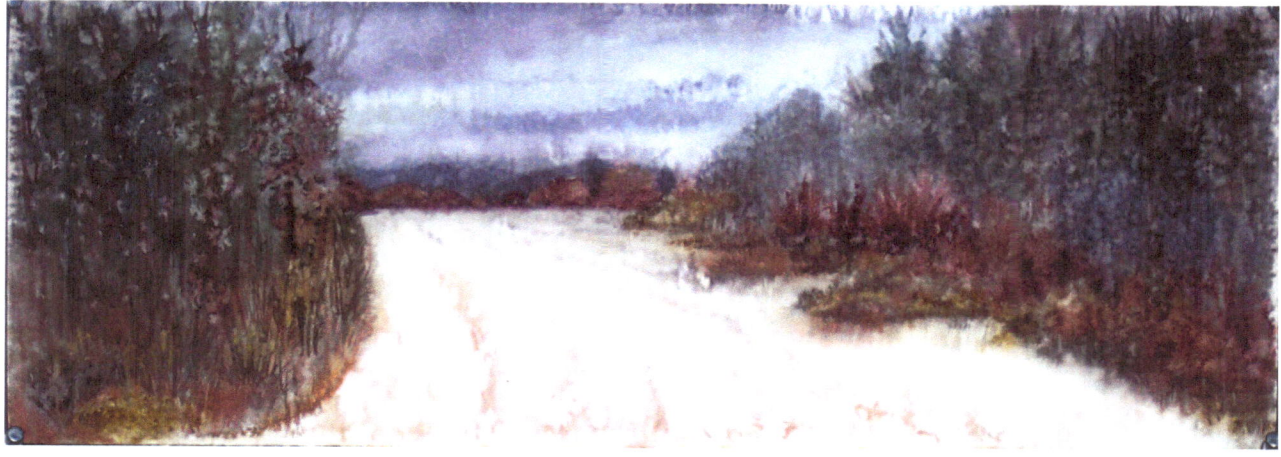

Winter Meadow, Watercolor on Masa Paper, 10.5x31"

Painting Basics

How do we begin? Have everything at the ready: water containers, filled spray bottle, paper and mounting board, brushes, a fully charged palette, three or four paper towels folded for the blotting of brushes, kosher salt and table salt.

Mount a sheet of masa as previously described, on which to practice the following techniques:

Flat wash: A painted area in which the paint is evenly applied. The easiest way to make a flat wash is to dampen the area, and then apply color and spread it out using a light touch to the area's boundaries.

Graded wash: A painted area within which the paint gradually becomes lighter from the edge of one portion to the edge of another portion. An example of this might be a cloudless, blue sky. Load your widest oval or flat wash brush with paint. You will need more paint than you might think, so really load up your brush. With as few strokes as possible, begin wherever you wish the darkest portion of the wash to be found. Apply a strip of indigo across the entire width of the paper starting at the top. Rinse your brush and lightly blot the bristles on a folded paper towel so as not to puddle

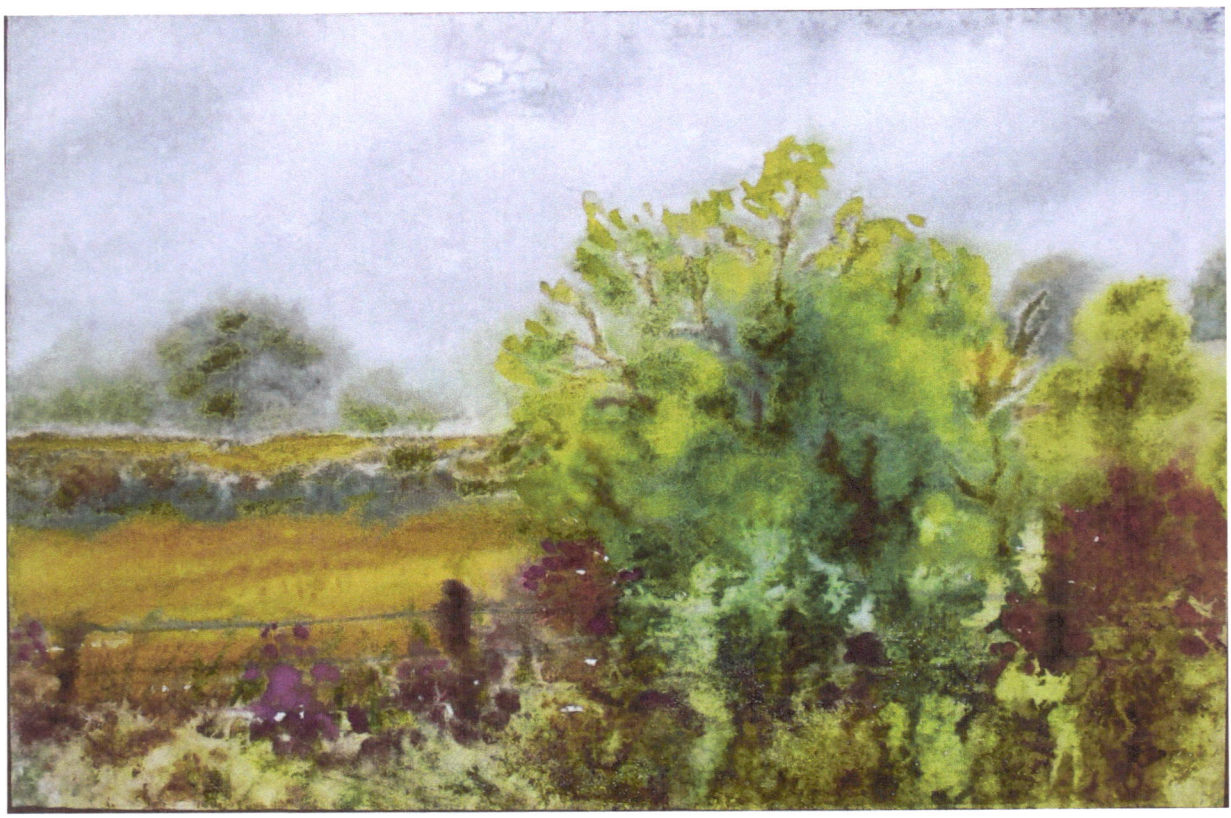

Rain, Drizzle, Fog, Watercolor on Masa Paper, 10.5x14"

the paper with excess water. A bead of water and paint should have begun to collect at the bottom edge of the indigo strip. If this is not happening, slightly elevate the support board to encourage that to happen. Now, take a fresh stroke with your clean, wet brush, catching the edge of the bead at the bottom edge of your first pass. Rinse and lightly blot your brush once again. Then, make a third pass in the same manner. Proceed in this way until you have painted all the way to the bottom edge of the region you intend for the graded wash, each time reducing the pigment while expanding the overall effect. You have just created a graded wash.

Backwash: Also known as a controlled bloom, this is a painted area in which the paint has been applied, allowed to dry slightly, and then a few drops of clean water are set into the wash. As the water drops spread, they push the pigment away from their centers, creating a shape paler in color than its surroundings. This technique is ideal for making cloud effects or rendering the leaf masses of shrubbery and trees. It's considered a fault in more conservative watercolor painting circles, yet it can be very effective when used with discretion.

Salted wash: A painted area in which the paint has been applied, allowed to dry slightly, and then "salted" by scattering or sprinkling salt on the surface. When the salt begins to dissolve, it pushes water and pigment away, creating a lighter spot for each granule of salt. Coarse-grained Kosher salt produces larger effects, while finer table salt imparts smaller effects. Timing is very important in getting the salt to work. The paper should be wet enough to have the look of satin. If very wet, the salt will just melt away into the excess water. If it is too dry, the salt will do nothing. The sudden appearance of the salt effect is almost magical as these delicate, almost lacey spots form. Be sparing in the application. A lot of salt does not do much more than a few grains.

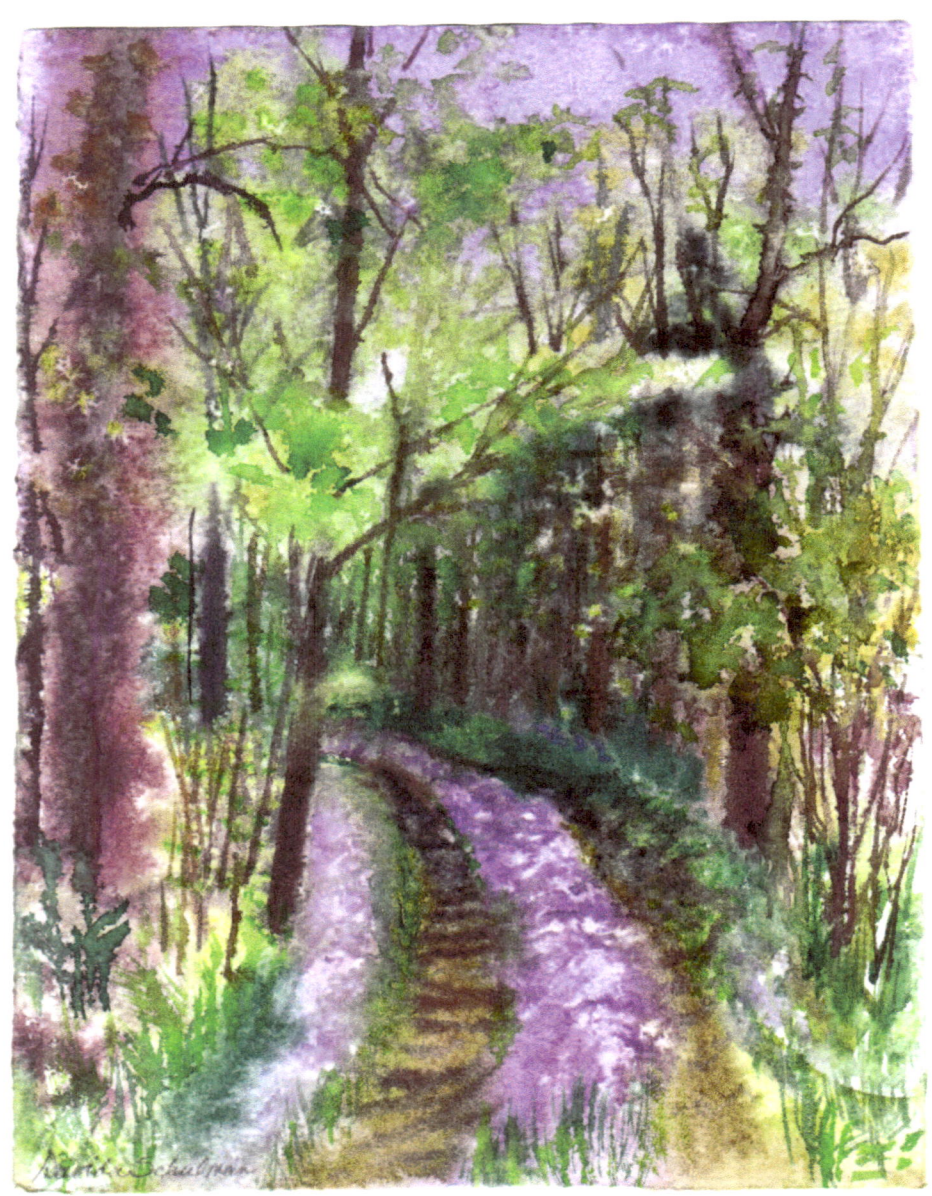

Forget-Me-Not Lane Watercolor on Masa Paper, 10.5x7"

Once you have practiced these techniques, you are ready to create your first watercolor painting.

What's there to paint? For several reasons, I like to teach beginners to start with a simple landscape painting. Landscapes require the use of all the basic techniques you have just practiced. They are not as dependent on the artist having highly developed drawing skills as other subject matter might be. Of course, working to enhance your drawing skills is always important in representational painting, but it's not mandatory. If you have confidence in your drawing skills, preliminary penciling can be abandoned for a direct-to-paint approach. I paint in this way.

I gradually abandoned the drawing stage for several reasons. Since watercolor is transparent, it will reveal even minimal penciling. Beginners typically tend to overdraw. They think that every detail must be in place before beginning to apply paint. Once the painting process has begun, the graphite from the drawing will go into suspension in the watercolor. It contaminates the transparent color, making it muddy. Also, the nature of masa paper's surface makes erasing pencil marks impossible without damage to the paper. I personally like the spontaneity of painting directly with no preliminary penciling. Any resulting surprises as the painting dries are part of the fun.

An inexpensive painting support, like masa paper, makes direct painting a lot less risky and frees the artist to take chances and play. Risk-taking is part of the process of growing as an artist. Yes, it's disappointing to have a work turn out in a way you don't like, but that's part of the learning experience. Failure can be a great teacher.

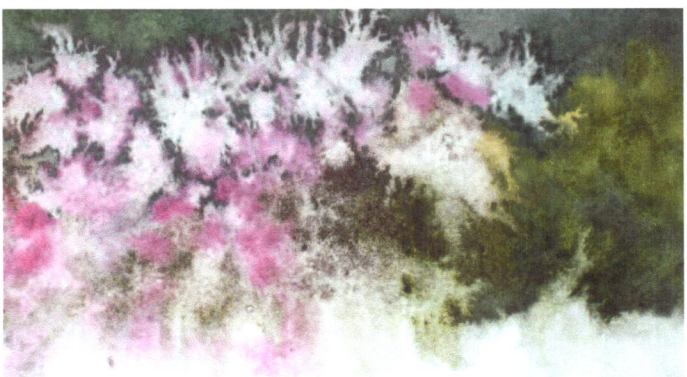

Salt in a wet wash can offer some pretty impressive effects. Done with coarse kosher salt. Once the wash is bone dry, brush the salt off and add color to the blooms.

A sample of a salted wash. If you look closely, you can see the grains of kosher salt.

A First Landscape

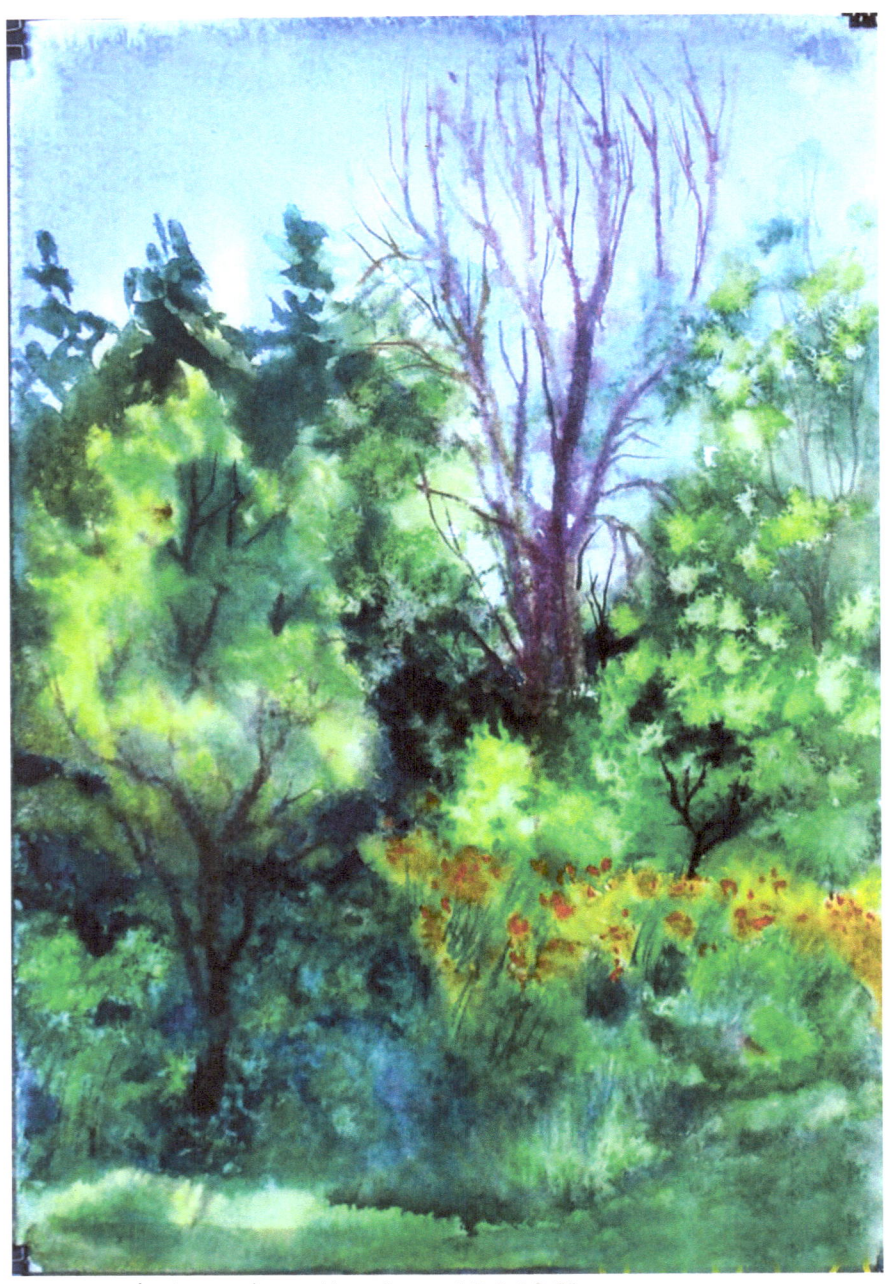

In My Woods, Watercolor on Masa Paper, 15.5x10.5"

If you imagine that all the small details; tree trunks, branches and flower blooms, have not been placed, what you have is a ground which is purely abstract. It is only when those small details have been applied that it all snaps into a believable landscape. This was a mode used by the master of the abstract ground, John Singer Sargent.

A note on white and tints:

Transparent watercolor has no white pigment. Any white in the painting is the white of the paper and must be preserved as you paint. Tints (e.g. pink is a tint of red) are created by the dilution of pigment with the addition of water. Use more water for pale, less-saturated color, and less water for stronger, more-saturated color.

Let's begin:

Lightly spray your palette colors with water if they have dried. Mount the paper as previously described. Place something under the top edge of the mounting board to prop it up at a slight angle so the water and paint will flow toward the bottom.

Begin with a graded wash to represent a blue sky. The sky has its deepest blue color directly overhead and gradually becomes pale toward the horizon. A graded wash is perfect for representing this phenomenon. The wash ends where you intend to place the horizon. For good composition, it should be above or below the halfway point from top to bottom.

Create the ground plane with another graded wash by mixing a dark green with yellow and blue with a touch of red. Starting just below your chosen horizon line, execute your second graded wash, continuing it to the bottom of the paper. You have just established a blue sky and a ground plane. The horizon line is the top edge of the green ground plane.

You might leave a very narrow band of white space between the sky and the ground plane. By narrow, I mean a very narrow, thread-like strip. This will help to prevent the two colors from bleeding into each other. This technique allows you to continue painting while controlling the spread of the paint from area to area. The tiny beads of white can be eliminated later or you may choose to leave them. It's a matter of taste.

As the graded washes become gradually paler with each stroke down the paper, the effect mimics the sky and the ground's perceived change of tone from dark to light as they become closer to the viewer. By imitating that perception on paper, they appear to "lay down" or spread out spatially like horizontal surfaces. If they are painted in one continuous tone, they are flat, perceived as a vertical wall rather than a horizontal plane.

It is important to complete the sky wash and ground plane washes quickly. You want to take advantage of the wet paper after the washes are complete. This will provide the soft, atmospheric effect for rendering objects in the distance. As the paper gets drier, you will begin to apply small finishing touches in the foreground that are crisper. This is kind of a dance. The challenge lies in balancing softness with the final, crisper bits of the painting.

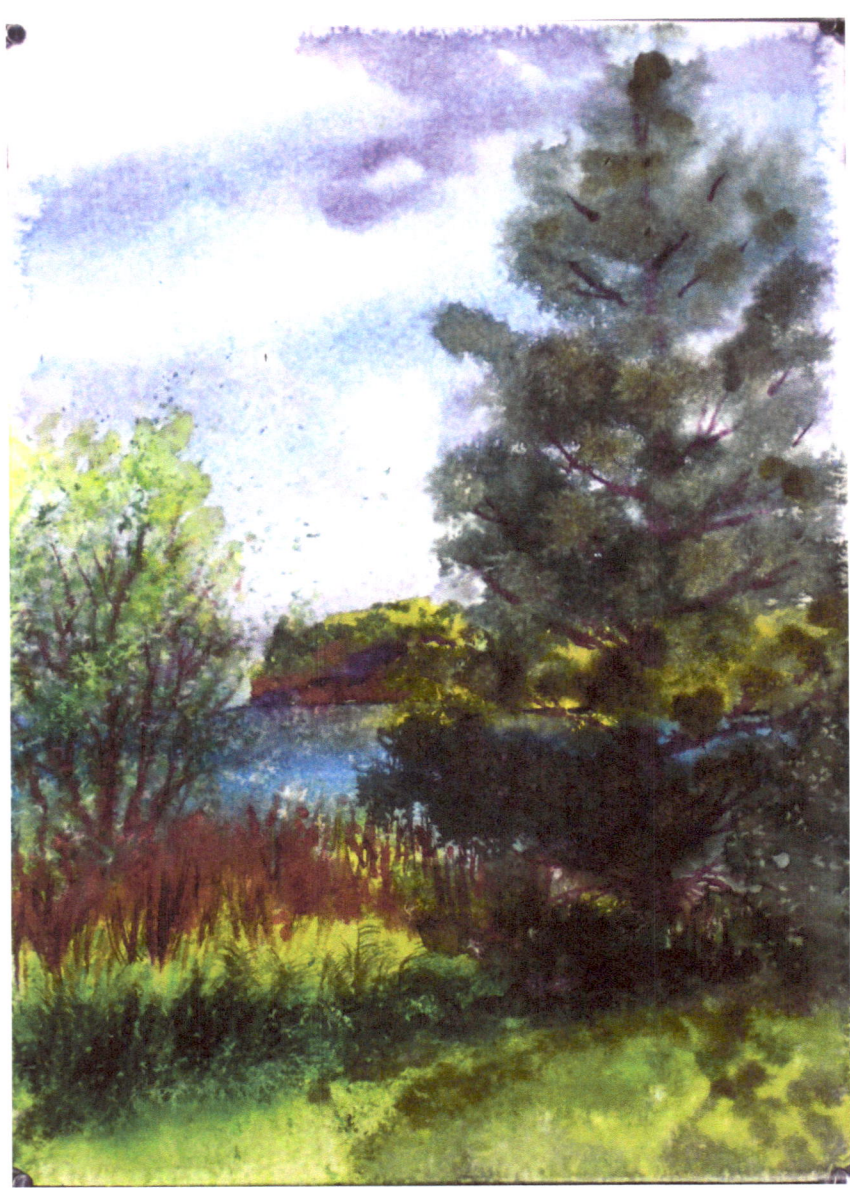

At the Lake Shore, Watercolor on Masa Paper, 15.5x10.5"
The openings in the tree on the right allow for the background information to be seen while providing spaces to indicate the branches of the tree.

Once the sky and ground planes have been established, you have a created an illusionistic space. The objects you paint in that space can appear to exist in a believable way. This is where an awareness of the difference in paint density plays a key role in the painting. It is these differences in proportional density that allow you paint one hue over another as long as the top color application is with a dense pigment.

The heaviness of that pigment will push the previous wet layer aside. It is also opaque enough to cover an already dry area. Mix a dark, gray green that is more blue than yellow. You are going to replicate a painting discovery made by Leonardo Da Vinci. He observed that color appears to gradually become more blue, more gray, and more pale on objects as they are at greater distance. This is now called atmospheric or aerial perspective. You will be placing objects of the greatest distance at the horizon, so they will need to the be bluest, grayest, and most pale greens. To make them a little more gray, add a small amount of red. It's the complement of green. If you mix complements, the colors become grayer.

Apply the green you just mixed at the horizon and slightly above it to form some background woods. These woods will be small because we perceive objects at greater distance to be smaller than objects at lesser distance. Remember to think of the roundness of leaf masses as you paint. Let your brush create irregular globules that will represent leaf masses at a distance. If you paint like you are painting a wall, that's what you'll get. Allow the paint to bleed into the wet sky to form a soft edge representing the branchy tops of the trees. You may apply this paint all the way across the paper or partially across the paper. It should be a little paler than the ground plane at the horizon. Your paint applications should become more intense and at a higher contrast as you paint your way out the painting. By that I mean it is logical and customary to paint background to foreground. However, you must establish ways of painting that are right for you. I suggest using this procedure as you begin, and as you gain experience with watercolors, you may modify your painting technique to suit your needs and the needs of each painting.

You are now ready to add foreground information. The easiest trees to paint are the conifers like pine and spruce. If you have seen Bob Ross paint, he almost exclusively paints conifers for precisely that reason. Keep in mind that conifers are cone-shaped. On paper, they become triangular. Some are squat and wide while others are elongated and tall. To give the look of three dimensions, their value must change from light on the sunlit side to dark on the shadow side. Also, the bottoms of the conifer fronds should be darker as their undersides are away from the light.

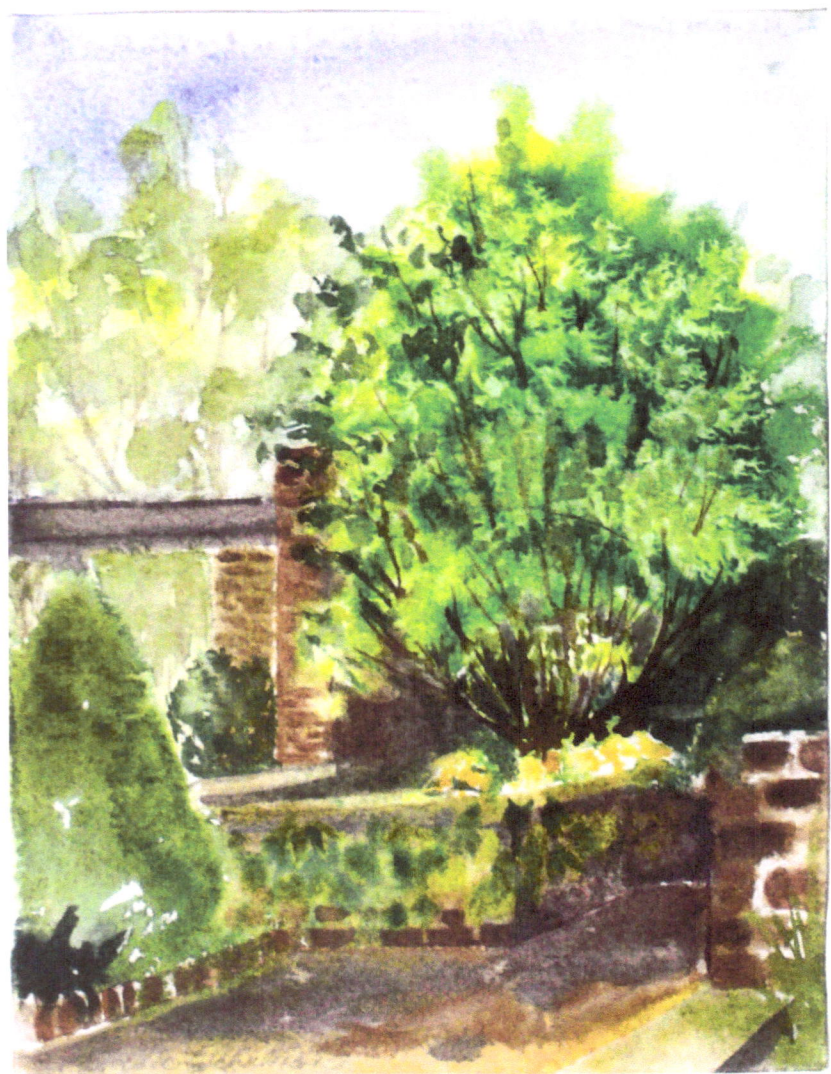

Gardens, Watercolor on Masa Paper, 10.5x14"
The 'leaves' on this tree were created with a salted wash using table salt. A layer of yellow green was put down first. After the yellow green had dried thoroughly a layer of darker green was put down. Salt was placed in the second layer creating leaf like forms by allowing the light layer to show through the darker wash.

Try to avoid painting them the way you did in third grade. You remember the drawings of Christmas trees with a fully visible central trunk and regular, downward angled strokes that are narrow at the apex and wider at the bottom? That is a beginner's tendency, especially if your art education ended in grade school. Whenever your exploration of art ended, your skills became frozen in time. Those drawings were not about what you saw. They remain more akin to a pictographic language such as Chinese characters. They are pictograms, hieroglyphics, more closely related to verbal thinking than to visual thinking.

Now, put the tree on the left or right of center. Also, make it tall enough to cross the horizon line. That will marry the sky portion with the rest of the ground plane and connect it with your foreground trees. Also, when you make clusters of anything, the clusters are more effective if they are in odd numbers, such as three, five or seven. Load your brush with a yellow-green. Begin at the top with the growing end of the tree. Those are the branches that poke skyward with a few small axial branches around them. Let your brush dance and skip around. The fronds on the left and right sides of the trees have bits that stick out in an irregular way while gradually expanding, becoming wider toward the bottom. Some fronds in front of the central trunk are pointing directly at you and you see them edge on. This is where the dancing and skipping of the brush provides bleeds, blobs and bloops. That, and the wetness of the paper, express the character of the needles of the coniferous tree.

Remind yourself not to fill in the tree solidly. You've taken great pains to create an environment for the pine trees to live in. Don't cover it all up! Remember, even pine trees are lacey. You can see things through the gaps in their foliage. By leaving gaps, you save space for a bit of sky or a branch to peak through the openings. If the paper is wet, you will need to space these tree elements farther apart than you think they should be, as the paint will spread on the wet surface

Paint with a light green color first. You can always add darks afterward while it is still wet. It is difficult to lighten an area once it has dried but, you can wring out your brush and lift some paint if it is still wet.

You have not painted any of the skeletal structure yet; no branches or trunks. So far you've only painted the greenery. Since the paint is transparent, painting the dark trunk and branches first would make all your painted foliage appear to be on the backside of the tree. You can add those portions of the trunk and branches that are visible between the gaps in the leaf masses afterward. Those are the details which will become part of the finishing touches.

Now, load your brush with a dark blue-green plus a little red to make it slightly grayer. Touch the areas that will represent shadow. Let the paint spread. Do this with some thought as to where the shadows should be in relation to your light source, the sun. Remember to leave those gaps!

Paint another tree and make it a smaller than the first one. Then, make another tree. Size it in between the sizes of the other two trees. Paint around the second tree to place the third tree behind it. Change the character of the green slightly with each tree you create by adding a little more of one color in your primary triad each time you paint a tree. This will help the viewer see the trees as separate elements. You may also wish to change the value (degree of lightness or darkness).

You are now ready to add the closest foreground information. This will help create the visual effect of a deeper space. The objects in the foreground should have the greatest contrast and the most saturated color. They should also reside within the palest tone of the graded wash you put down earlier. Read the description of a salted wash described earlier. If the area has dried, gently re-wet the paper with a light misting

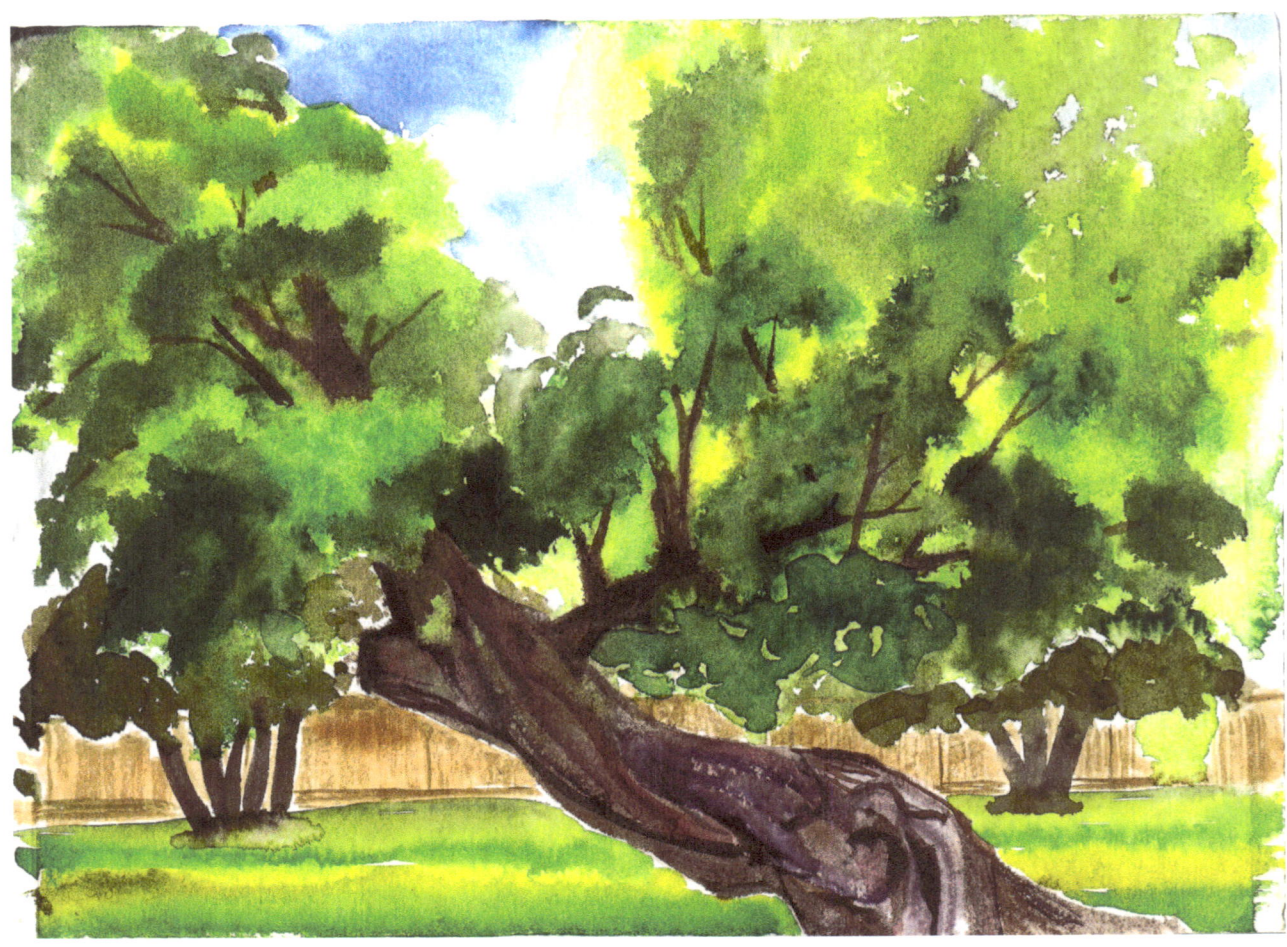

Old Box Elder, Watercolor on Masa Paper, 7.5x10.5"

of water. Place a deep green on the damp surface and wait until the surface begins to look like satin. Take a pinch of kosher salt or table salt and sprinkle it on the area. The magic of the salt will happen suddenly. If you look away for a few moments, you'll miss it. The salt wash is a trick every watercolor painter knows. Use it selectively and only if the painting calls for it; not just for the sake of using it.

While you are waiting for the salt to work, use a rigger to poke the branches you wish to show between into the gaps you have left in the trees. (The long bristles of the rigger hold a lot of paint. This allows you to long fine lines which gradually narrow as the paint is deposited. It imitates the growth pattern of small tree branches from broad to narrow.) Then, when your salted wash is thoroughly dry, you can place color in the spots created by the salt. Brush any remaining salt off the painting before adding color. You may also add grasses and branches in the foreground. Try not to obsess. We all have a tendency to pick at our paintings, thinking they need something here or there, when in actuality, the painting is done and what we are adding does nothing more for it. It's best to put it aside and not look at it again for a few days. Only then will you be able to see it with fresh eyes. That's art making at its best. At its worst, we may ruin it by overworking.

Congratulations! You have now completed your first landscape watercolor without sweating the details.

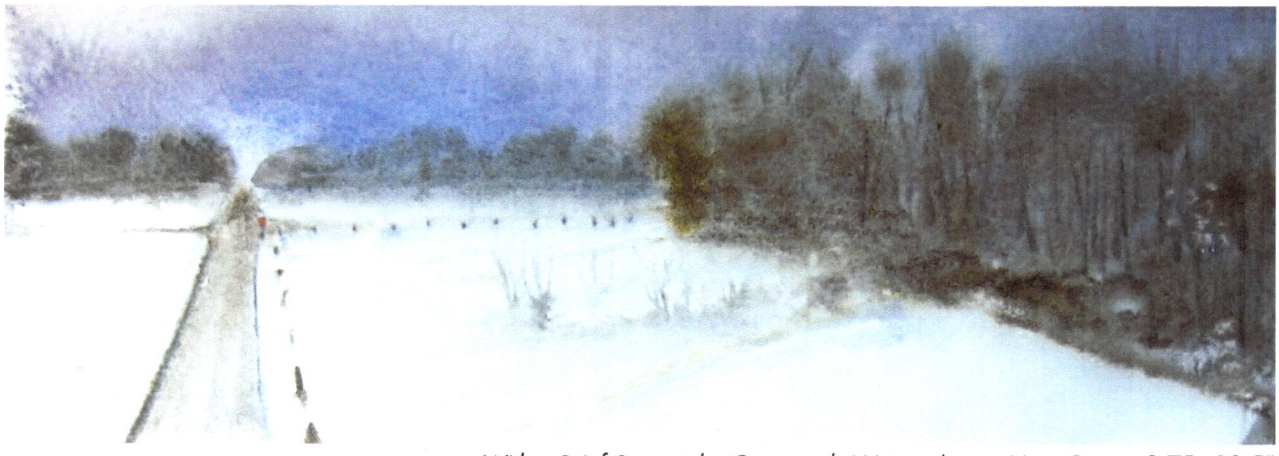

With a Brief Stop at the Crossroad, Watercolor on Masa Paper, 3.75 x10.5"

A First Still Life

A still life is the next hurdle in your introduction to watercolor painting. Before making a still life, gain some experience with watercolor by painting a few landscapes. It will familiarize you with the materials of this new medium and provide you with an idea of what to expect from your personal approach. When selecting the objects for painting, remember to choose something that is within your artistic capability. You want this to be challenging enough to allow you to grow, but not so far beyond your capability that you end up frustrated.

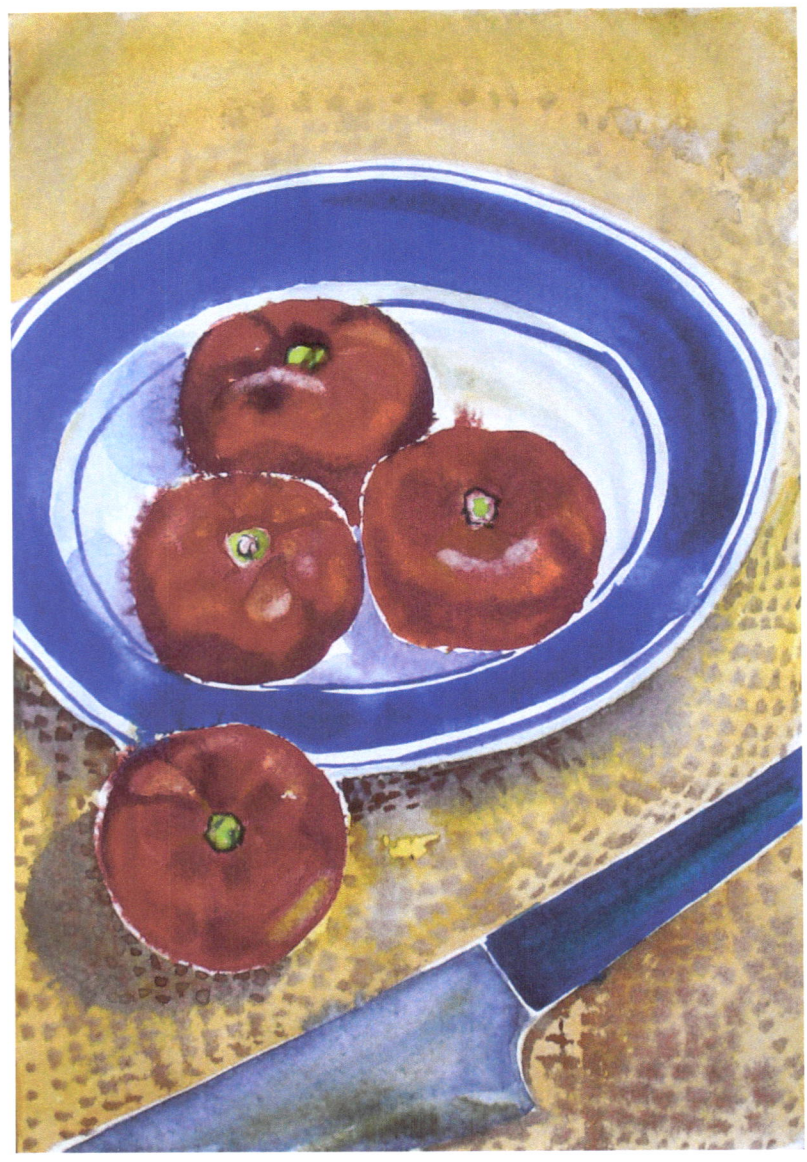

Home Grown, Watercolor on Masa Paper, 15.5x10.5"

This a good still life composition for a beginner to paint. But please set up your own. It is not a good idea to copy another work or to copy a photograph.

You learn nothing from that practice. All the work of translating three dimensional objects to a two dimensional surface has been done for you. It's far more important to learn how to do that for yourself.

Set up your still life with care. Select a few pieces of fruit or some vegetables. Three is a good number to be included with some crockery, a cup or a bowl. If you select a bowl for your fruit and veggies, put some of them in the bowl and some outside of the bowl. This is for compositional reasons. Placing all of the fruit in the bowl will visually merge them into a single object. If that's all you place on the paper, you will have an isolated object which has no relationship to the field (the surface and the edge of the paper). It becomes a kind of bull's eye that keeps the viewer looking only in one place since there is no other place to look. By having at least three objects, you can connect them to the edges of the paper and overlap them to establish a sense of space. It creates a relationship with the field and other objects in the picture. This allows the eye to travel around the painting by providing something of interest in different places.

Consider the contrasts in color and the values in your arrangement. If you take time to think about your setup in terms of color and value, it will have a direct effect on the result. It takes me a long time to set up a still life. I'll put things in place and leave them for a day or two. I'll alter positions. I'll swap things out. I'll change fabrics. I'll fiddle with the lighting. Doing all of these things makes the actual painting proceed more smoothly.

This is also the time to think about drawing skill. A still life demands greater drawing skills than a landscape. You must observe well. The fruit and vegetable forms are deceptively simple, yet their shapes are very specific. For instance, a Delicious apple has a very different shape than a Macintosh apple. Peppers have lobes which form their shapes, and those shapes can vary widely from pepper to pepper. You still are free to use artistic license. You are not a camera, and your audience will have no idea what you assembled for still life or exactly what it looked like. Was it an apple or a plum? It doesn't matter. All you need to do is make it believable. You do not need to go through the contortions to make your painting of fruit exactly as you've seen it.

I don't sketch anything when I paint. But, I have been doing this for a long time. So if you need to pencil, do so, but do it minimally so the graphite doesn't contaminate your color. Also, with your pencil on a piece of sketch paper, make a small value study. Small means no larger than 4"x 6". Use only three values: black, white and one gray. This will help you with placement and provide a roadmap which will help you locate your darkest darks and your lightest lights. If you make a line drawing without providing whole areas of value, you are doing yourself a disservice. A line drawing does not provide enough information to be an effective guide for painting.

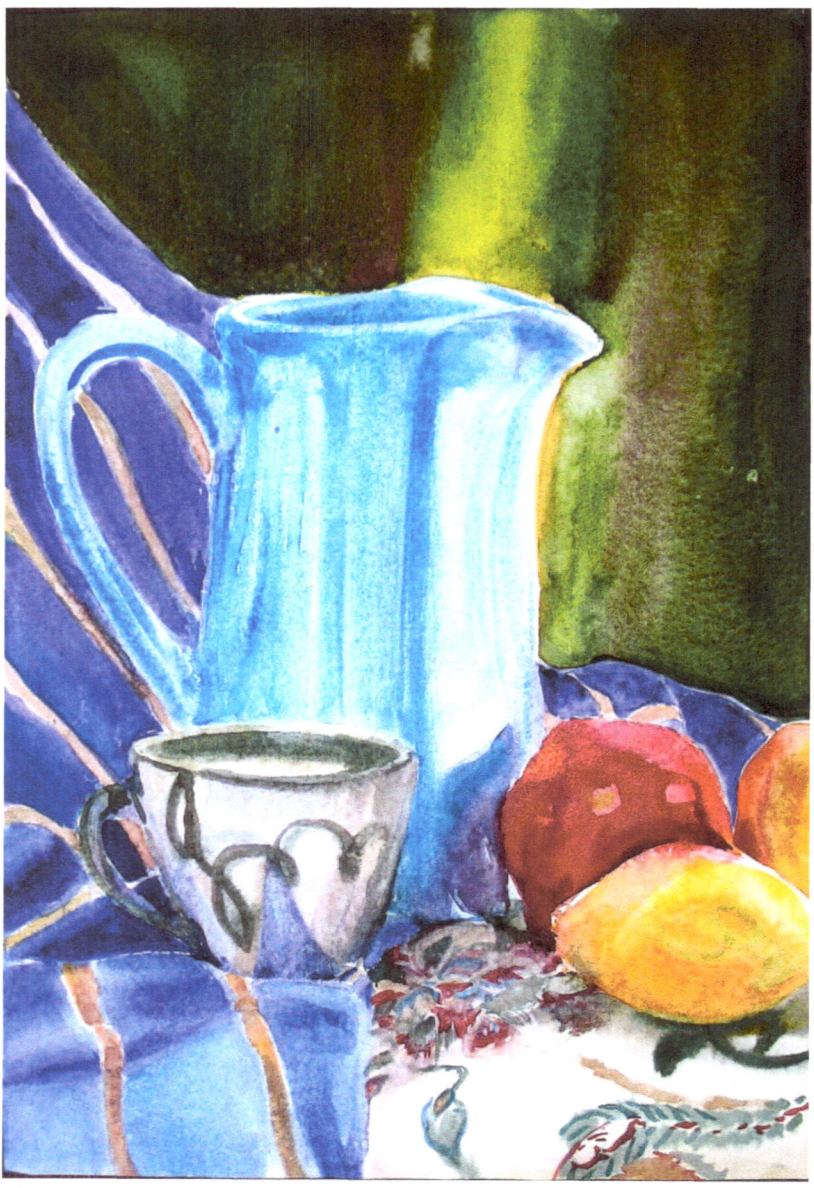

Blue Jug with Fruit, Watercolor on Masa Paper, 15.5x10.5"

A value study is not a detailed drawing. It is a generalized step and should take no more than ten minutes to complete. It should focus on large areas of value with very little or no attention paid to detail. Remember, the point is not to sweat the details! Once you make your value study, refer to it while you are working. We typically tend to forget about it once we become immersed in the painting process. Keep the value study visible within your work area so you can follow the plan that it represents. You may always deviate from it if the painting seems to require it.

If you need to indicate the locations of each object on your paper, lightly pencil in their positions. Remember that penciling in transparent watercolor should be kept to a minimum. Your value study will guide you to completion. Make sure you have good lighting. Fluorescent lights illuminating your subject matter are the worst for painting and for drawing because the light is too diffuse. A strong, single-point source of light on your subject from one specific direction is ideal. If that light is strong enough, it will swamp the diffuse light of a fluorescent source. Better yet, turn off the fluorescent lights.

Now that you have made your preparations, it's time to think about an execution strategy. Since I don't pencil, I paint from foreground to background. The tomatoes in the painting shown were painted first. I used a warm, orange-red to establish the shapes of each tomato before adding cooler, bluer reds for the shadows when the wash was still wet. I created highlights by wringing my brush out so it was nearly dry. I then used it to lift color out for highlights. Masa paper really facilitates lifting color when the paint is wet.

The fine white lines around the tomatoes served as barriers to keep the wet colors from bleeding uncontrollably into one another. Some bleeds, like those around the edges of the tomatoes, are something I personally like. It's an acknowledgement of the fluid nature of watercolor. The softness enforces the illusion that the tomatoes on the flat surface are spheroid and the surfaces are tucking themselves away, around, and under the bottom of each tomato.

After completing that portion, I painted the broad blue stripe of the plate rim while painting around the upper edge of the tomatoes overlapping the plate. Then, came the narrow stripes. I placed some dark blues into the stripe where the shadows should be and used a pale blue-violet for the shadows cast by the tomatoes on the plate. It is always a good idea to remember that shadows are not black. They are merely the same color as their surroundings but a darker, grayer shade. You can create shadow tones by adding the complementary color of a shadowed object to gray and darken the color, or you can use an analogous color—a color on the color wheel situated on either side of the base color of the object you intend to represent. An analogous color will only alter temperature and will not gray the color.

For instance, the base color of the tomatoes was cadmium red light, which is an orange red. I used cadmium red deep for the shadow, which is cooler by virtue of its slightly bluer character. Finally, I used a violet red for the very deepest tones of the tomatoes. As for the tablecloth on which all this sits, I selected a yellow that was orange enough to make the blue appear more intense and yellow enough to intensify the violets in the tomatoes.

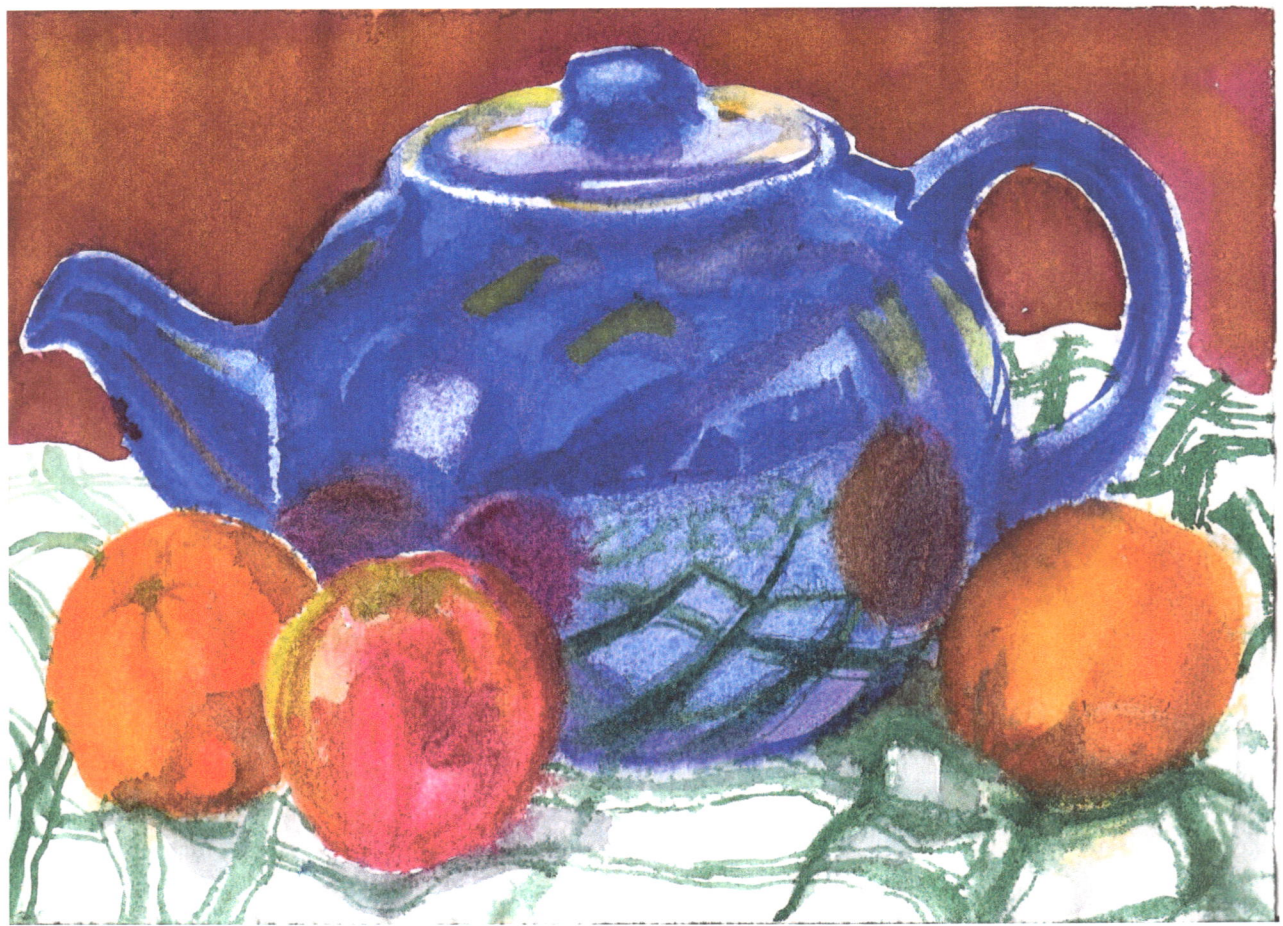

Teapot Reflections, Watercolor on Masa Paper, 7.5x10.5"

The shadows cast on the tablecloth are a mixture proceeding from yellow to a dominant violet. Shadows cast by objects are darker when closest to the objects which cast them. These shadows become paler and their edges fade away as their distance from the objec⁻ increases. This principle is evident in the darkness of the tablecloth pattern within the shadows created by the plate and the knife. The tablecloth pattern becomes less distinct and fades away at the top of the painting. This imitates the ground plane of a landscape. It makes the table top lay down as a horizontal plane in the same manner. The final touch is the green of the tomato stems, which also helps intensify the reds of the tomatoes.

This is my take on a simple still life. Yours will no doubt be different, but this will give you an idea of what to keep in mind when you are painting. Many of these tips will come to mind naturally as you gain experience. That's when you will need to find something a little more challenging to paint in order to continue your evolution as an artist.

Play and experiment. Take risks. Masa paper allows you to do that without breaking your bank account. A time will come when you might choose to move on to other materials. I took up oil painting in addition to watercolors. But watercolor is my medium of first choice because of its portability and capacity to achieve stunning effects within seconds rather than hours.

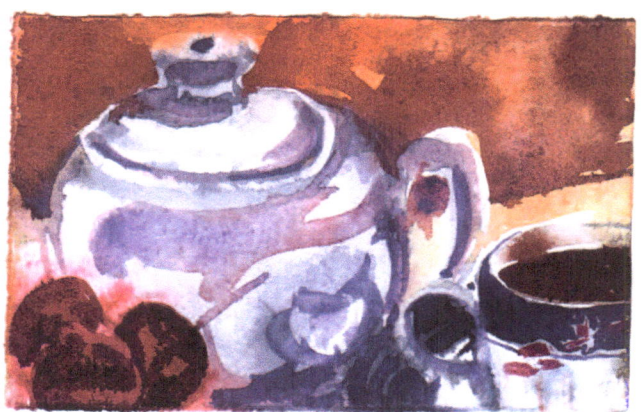

Small Still Life with Teapot, Watercolor on Masa Paper, 4x6.5"

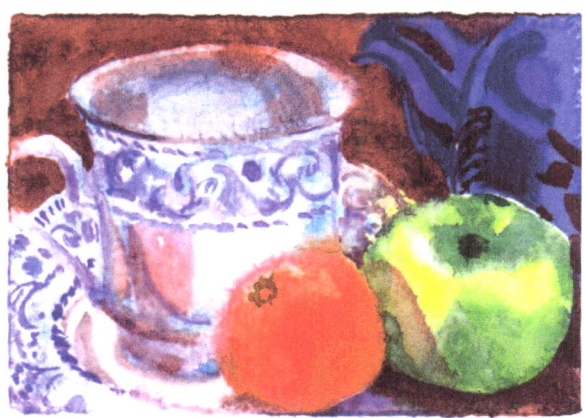

Small Still Life with Fruit, Watercolor on Masa Paper, 4x6"

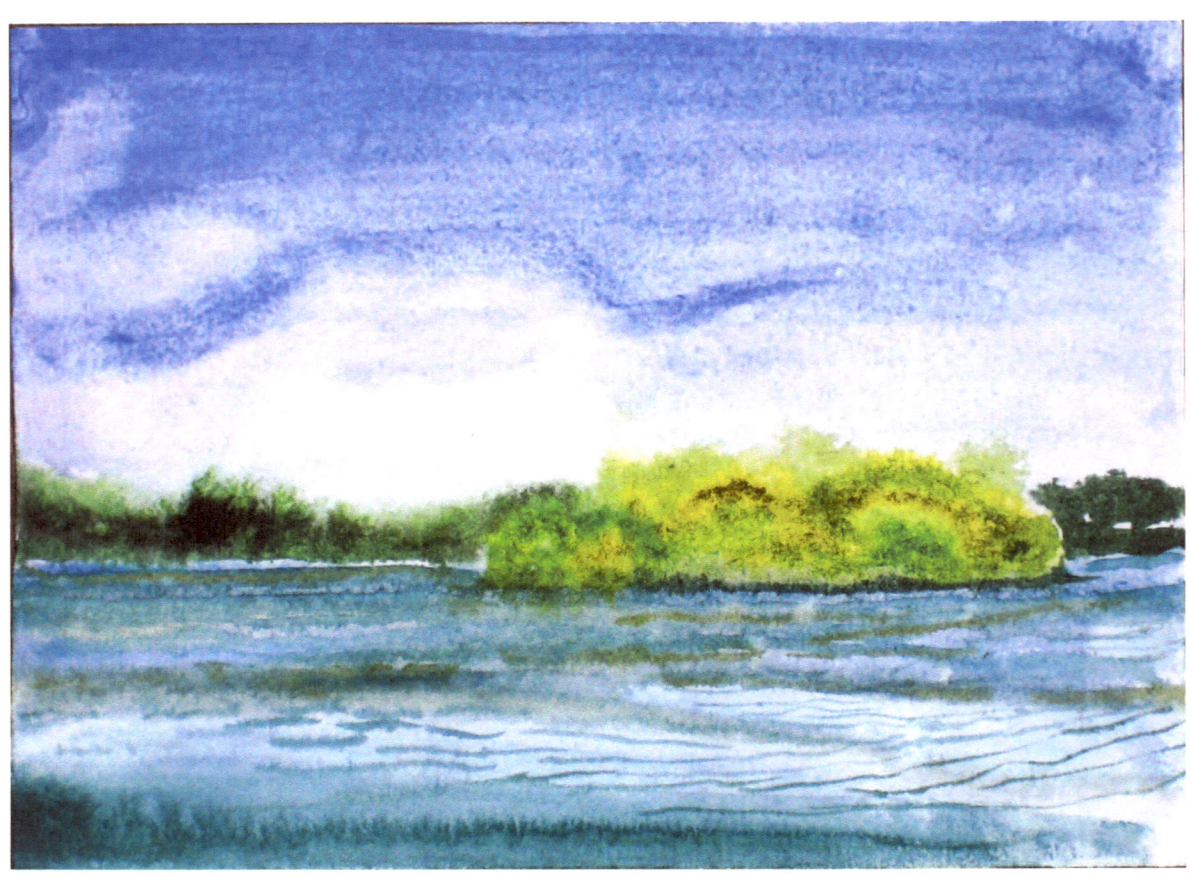

North Shore, Watercolor on Masa Paper, 5.75 x 3.75"

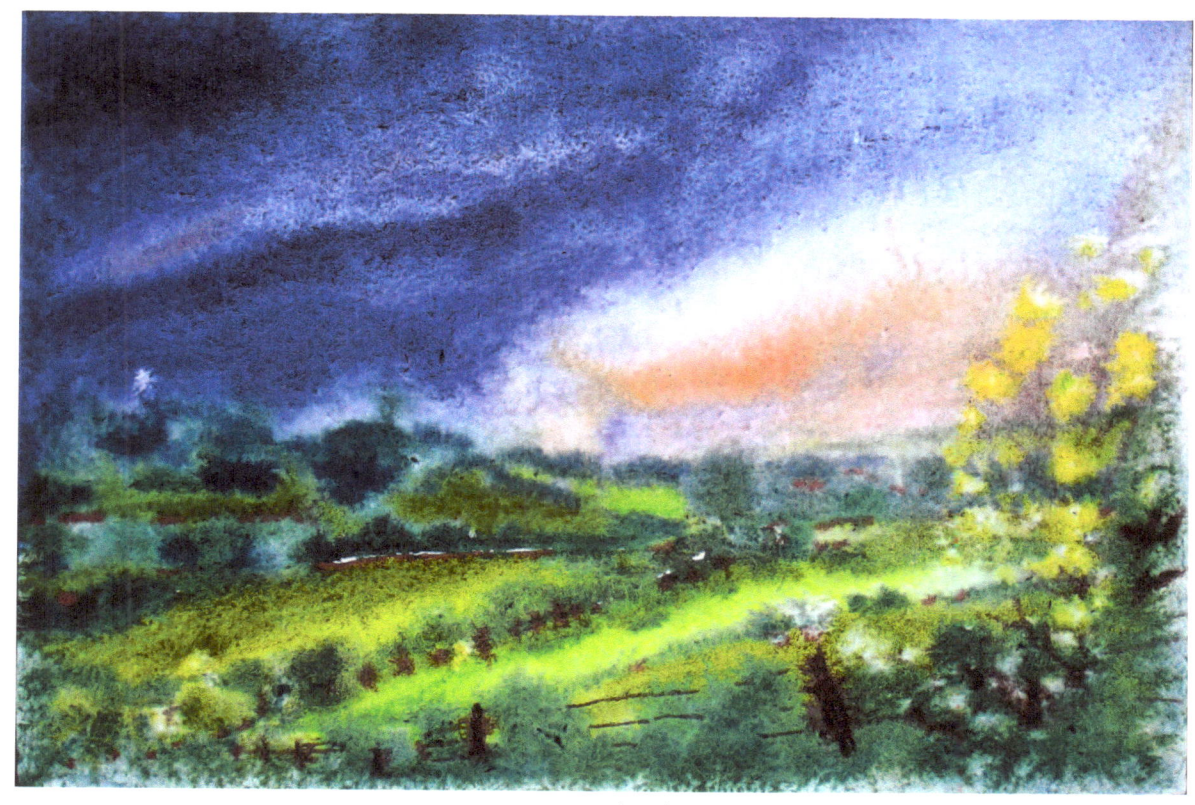

Passing Thunderstorm, Watercolor on Masa Paper, 10.5 x 14.5"

As you can see, the paper was quite wet throughout the whole painting process.

Resources

Local Art Supplies

The Artists' Guild**
215 N 3rd Ave
Sturgeon Bay, WI 54235
920-743-9900

Paint Box Gallery and Art Supply
10426 Highway 42
Ephraim, WI 54221
920-854-4435

Tradewinds Art and Framing Supplies
536 Greene Ave
Green Bay, WI 54301
920-432-0270

Mail Order Art Supplies:

Dick Blick*
DickBlick.com

Cheap Joes's Art Stuff*
cheapjoes.com
1848 Galleria Blvd,Ste D
Charlotte, NC 28270
704-845-2527

Daniel Smith
danielsmith.com

Jerry's Artarama*
jerrysartarama.com
800-827-8478

Art Supply Warehouse*
artsupplywarehouse.com
6672 Westminster Blvd.
Westminster, CA 92683
800.854.6467

Educational Resources:

Northest Wisconsin Technical College
nwtc.edu
NWTC Artisan and Business Center
1417 Cedar St, Green Bay, WI 54302
920-544-5018

Art Garage
theartgarage.org
1400 Cedar St
Green Bay, WI 54302
920-448-6800

Art Guilds and Leagues

Door County Art League
doorcountyartleague.org

Green Bay Artists' Colony
greenbayartcolony.com

Museums:

Art Institute of Chicago
111 S. Michigan Ave.
Chicago, IL 60603, USA
www.artic.edu

Hardy Gallery
thehardy.org
P.O. Box 394
Ephraim, WI 54211
920.854.2210

Miller Museum
millerartmuseum.org
107 South 4th Avenue
Sturgeon Bay, WI 54235

Minneapolis Institute of Art
new.artsmia.org
2400 Third Avenue South,
Minneapolis, MN 55404

Milwaukee Art Museum
700 N. Art Museum Drive
Milwaukee, WI 53202

Neville Museum
nevillepublicmuseum.org
210 Museum Place
Green Bay, WI 54303
920-448-4460

Hamilton Wood Type & Printing Museum
woodtype.org
1816 10th St
Two Rivers, WI 54241
920-794-6272

Magazines

Artists' Magazine
artistsnetwork.com

Watercolor Artist
watercolorartistmagazine.com

International Artists' Magazine
internationalartist.com

Framing Supplies:

The Artists' Guild
215 N 3rd Ave
Sturgeon Bay, WI 54235
920-743-9900

Paint Box Gallery and Art Supply
10426 Highway 42
Ephraim, WI 54221
920-854-4435

Tradewinds Art and Framing Supplies
536 Greene Ave
Green Bay, WI 54301
920-432-0270

* Indicates a resource for masa paper

** A resource for masa paper which has a more absorbant surface finish.

Notes

Notes

www.ingramcontent.com/pod-product-compliance
Lightning Source LLC
Chambersburg PA
CBHW050834180526
45159CB00004B/1902